HOW THINGS WORK

MEDICINE

COVER

*A healthy human heart—about the size of a closed fist—pumps an
average of 1,500 gallons of blood each day throughout the body,
beating more than 2.8 billion times during a lifetime. Treating heart
disease is one of modern medicine's greatest challenges.*

HOW THINGS WORK

MEDICINE

TIME-LIFE BOOKS

ALEXANDRIA, VIRGINIA

Library of Congress Cataloging-in-Publication Data

Medicine
        p.   cm.   – (How things work)
    Includes index.
    ISBN 0-8094-7870-6 (trade)
    ISBN 0-8094-7871-4 (lib.)
    1. Medicine. Popular
    I. Time-Life Books.   II. Series.
    RC81.M4957   1991
    610—dc20   90-26963
                            CIP

How Things Work was produced by
ST. REMY PRESS

PRESIDENT	Pierre Léveillé
PUBLISHER	Kenneth Winchester

Staff for *MEDICINE*

Editor	Daniel McBain
Art Director	Normand Boudreault
Assistant Editor	Megan Durnford
Contributing Editor	George Daniels
Research Editor	Fiona Gilsenan
Researcher	Hayes Jackson
Picture Editor	Chris Jackson
Designer	Chantal Bilodeau
Illustrators	Maryse Doray, Nicolas Moumouris, Robert Paquet, Maryo Proulx
Index	Christine M. Jacobs

Staff for *HOW THINGS WORK*

Series Editor	Carolyn Jackson
Senior Art Director	Diane Denoncourt
Senior Editor	Elizabeth Cameron
Researcher	Nyla Ahmad
Administrator	Natalie Watanabe
Production Manager	Michelle Turbide
Coordinator	Dominique Gagné
Systems Coordinator	Jean-Luc Roy

Time-Life Books Inc. is a wholly owned subsidiary of
THE TIME INC. BOOK COMPANY

President and Chief	Kelso F. Sutton
President, Time Inc. Books Direct	Christopher T. Linen

TIME-LIFE BOOKS INC.

Managing Editor	Thomas H. Flaherty
Director of Editorial Resources	Elise D. Ritter-Clough
Director of Photography and Research	John Conrad Weiser
Editorial Board	Dale Brown, Roberta Conlan, Laura Foreman, Lee Hassig, Jim Hicks, Blaine Marshall, Rita Mullin, Henry Woodhead
PUBLISHER	Joseph J. Ward
Associate Publisher	Trevor Lunn
Editorial Director	Donia Steele
Marketing Director	Regina Hall
Director of Design	Louis Klein
Supervisor of Quality Control	James King

Editorial Operations

Production	Celia Beattie
Library	Louise D. Forstall
Correspondents	Elisabeth Kraemer-Singh (Bonn); Christina Lieberman (New York); Maria Vincenza Aloisi (Paris); Ann Natanson (Rome).

THE WRITERS

Gord Bagley works as a freelance science writer. He is the founding editor of *Clinical Diagnostics Today*, a magazine dedicated to diagnostic medicine.

Frederic Golden is a science and medicine writer based in San Francisco. A former assistant managing editor of *Discover*, he has also served as the science and medicine editor of *Time* magazine.

Frann Harris is a freelance writer, specializing in medical, scientific and technical topics. Her articles have appeared in Canadian magazines, newspapers, and medical journals such as *Family Practice*.

Nicolas Regush is a medical journalist at the Montreal *Gazette*. He has worked as a consultant on bioethical issues at the Clinical Research Institute of Montreal and as a medical analyst for Canadian radio.

Richard Sutherland is a Montreal science writer who contributes to *The Medical Post* and *The Canadian Medical Association Journal*.

THE CONSULTANTS

Peter Morgan, MD, a former editor of *The Canadian Medical Association Journal*, is currently working as a consultant, researcher and writer in the health field. He has been a member of the faculty of medicine at McGill University and the University of Toronto.

Seymour Perry, MD, is the Chairman of the Department of Community and Family Medicine at the Georgetown University School of Medicine. He has also conducted research at the U.S. National Cancer Institute and served as Director of the Nation Center for Heath Care Technology.

For information about any Time-Life book, please write:
Reader Information
Time-Life Customer Service
P.O. Box C-32068
Richmond, Virginia
23261-2068

CONTENTS

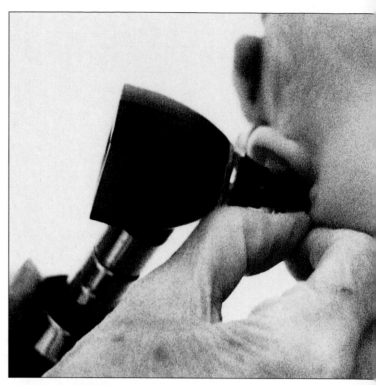

An otoscope is used to examine the ear.

Drug pellets tumble from an opened capsule.

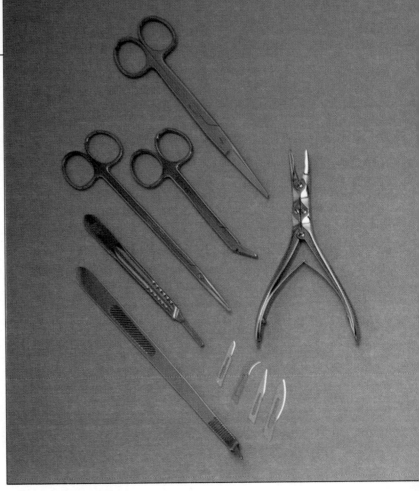

Tools employed in surgery.

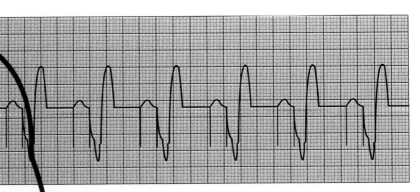

The heart pacemaker at work.

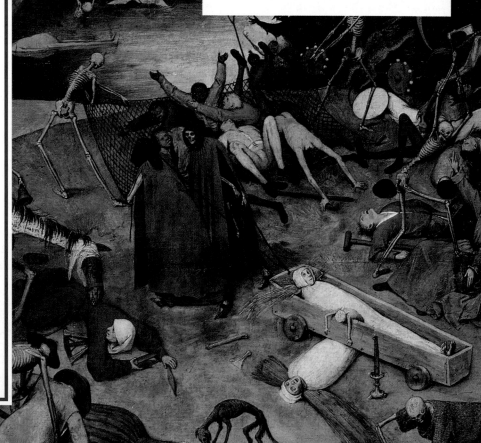

Medicine Meets Science

The history of medicine follows a tortuous route, from colorful ancient myths that attempted to explain disease to the astounding capabilities of medicine today. The art of healing underwent a significant transformation in roughly the 4th Century B.C., adopting a rational, scientific approach to the diagnosis and treatment of disease. At the forefront of this new philosophy was a compassionate and methodical Greek doctor named Hippocrates, believed to have contributed to an influential collection of books called the *Corpus Hippocraticum*—Hippocratic Collection. While the methods and theories in this collection appear rudimentary today, their insistence on acute observation and the interpretation of physical evidence were revolutionary, providing the logical base upon which modern medicine rests.

Yet, despite the lucid reasoning of the *Corpus*—and in similar early works by the Egyptians and the Chinese—a conspicuous gap in its teachings is a sound knowledge of the human body. The young sciences of anatomy and physiology remained cloaked in speculation through the Greco-Roman period and much of the medieval era, as religious and moral edicts forbidding human dissection forced pioneer researchers to make educated guesses. Even when the 14th Century brought increased dissection of human corpses—with or without official sanction—often doctors were only capable of seeing what they had already learned from the texts of Galen, a 2nd-Century Greek scientist whose human anatomy studies had been based on animal models.

Bruegel's Triumph of Death *(c. 1556) captures the horror of the bubonic plague. Known as the* Black Death, *the disease decimated Europe after being introduced to Italy by Crusaders returning from Crimea in 1348.*

Hippocrates, the "Father of Medicine," is regarded as the most influential medical teacher in history. Thought to have lived between 460 and 355 B.C., he wrote and compiled contemporary works on the art of healing.

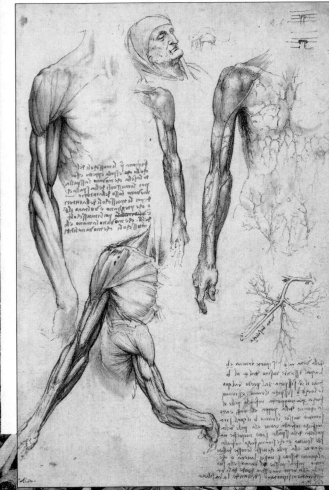

Perhaps the most enduring of all medical misconceptions was the Greek notion that health depended on the proper balance of four liquid elements, or humors: blood, phlegm, yellow bile and black bile. Each was associated with a dominant organ and a certain personality type, as illustrated below. Even though Leonardo da Vinci sketched very accurate anatomical drawings in the 15th Century (left), doctors still had much to learn about the human body.

Blood

Heart : Cheerful

Phlegm

Brain : Unexcitable

Black bile

Spleen : Depressive

Yellow bile

Liver : Hot-tempered

Medical Renaissance

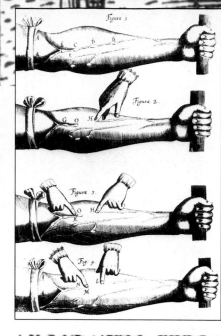

Science flourished in the 16th and 17th Centuries, as the Protestant Reformation permitted ideas that the medieval church would have condemned as heresy. Anatomists explored the human body in ever-greater depth, and the adventurous minds of the European Renaissance embraced theories that—while often seeming as incredible as medieval superstitions—were to prove scientifically viable.

A new explanation of infection, for example, was proposed by the Italian physician Girolamo Fracastoro; he hypothesized that plagues were carried by agents—invisible to the eye. Although he had no means of verifying the existence of these microorganisms, Fracastoro's theory was correct.

Physicians were repositories of an ever-increasing body of knowledge. With their new learning, doctors demanded higher fees for their services, and often catered to a wealthy urban clientele; sick people from poor and rural populations took their illnesses to apothecaries or to barbers whose services included surgery.

Forerunners of modern-day pharmacists, early apothecaries were grocers who also stocked the herbs, spices and minerals prescribed by doctors. Barber-surgeons, after a long tradition outside the margins of respectable medicine, applied the scientific knowledge of the day to ailments such as fractures, wounds, tumors and skin disease. Battlefield emergencies spawned a number of surgical innovations, and the textbook *A Universal Surgery*, by the French Army surgeon Ambroise Paré, elevated the practice to a new level of effectiveness.

This woodcut, from the surgical text Opus Chirurgicum, *suggests the vigorous atmosphere in a Renaissance hospital. Whereas physicians had traditionally taken their apprenticeship exclusively in universities, hospitals were becoming an increasingly important training ground.*

Today's understanding of the circulation of blood was first presented to the medical world in 1628, when William Harvey published On the Movement of the Heart and Blood in Animals, *from which the woodcut (left) is extracted. The illustration was used to prove the complementary role of arteries and veins. Ceramic apothecary jars such as this one, from 16th-Century Italy* (right), *contained increasingly exotic drugs as travel increased between Europe, Asia and the Americas.*

The practice of surgery made great strides during the Renaissance, both in technique and respectability. This page (right) from a later surgical text illustrates techniques of mastectomy, as well as displaying some of the instruments employed.

Fighting the Invisible Enemy

With the late-17th-Century invention of the microscope, by Dutch experimenter Anthony van Leeuwenhoek, doctors could see visual evidence of the existence of bacteria; the role of these microbes as agents of contagious disease remained to be proven. While advances continued on all fronts of medicine—the development of anesthesia, for example—many breakthroughs during the next two centuries related to infection.

The combined work of three individuals clarified the relationship between microscopic invaders—such as the smallpox virus—and infection. Louis Pasteur, a French chemist, first ascribed biochemical actions, such as putrefaction, to bacteria. British surgeon Joseph Lister, who used sterilization to kill microorganisms in the operating room, reduced the ravages of surgical infection. And Robert Koch, a German doctor, spearheaded the identification of specific bacteria associated with communicable diseases.

The development of the smallpox vaccination stands as one of the most important medical achievements of all time. Until the English physician Edward Jenner courageously vaccinated a healthy boy with noxious matter from a cowpox pustule—thereby putting the immune system on guard against other poxes—this disfiguring and often fatal virus had taken a dreadful toll.

Medical science had made great strides since the days of Hippocrates, laying the groundwork for even more astonishing innovations in diagnosis and restorative treatment. Today, on the eve of the 21st Century, medicine's progress is no less astounding.

Two pillars of modern surgery, anesthesia and sterile technique, can be observed in this early 20th-Century operating room: An anesthesiologist holds a gauze mask containing anesthetic, and all members are dressed in sterile garb. Despite these advances, questionable patent medicines, such as the French anemia cure (above left), *grew in popularity.*

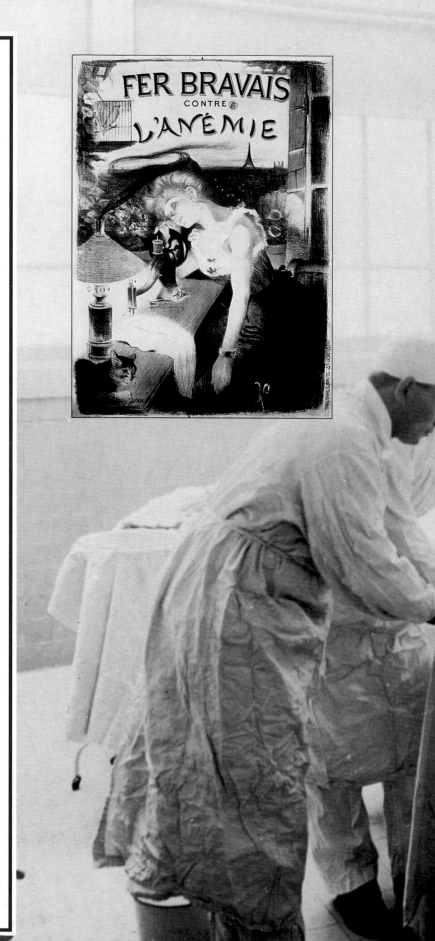

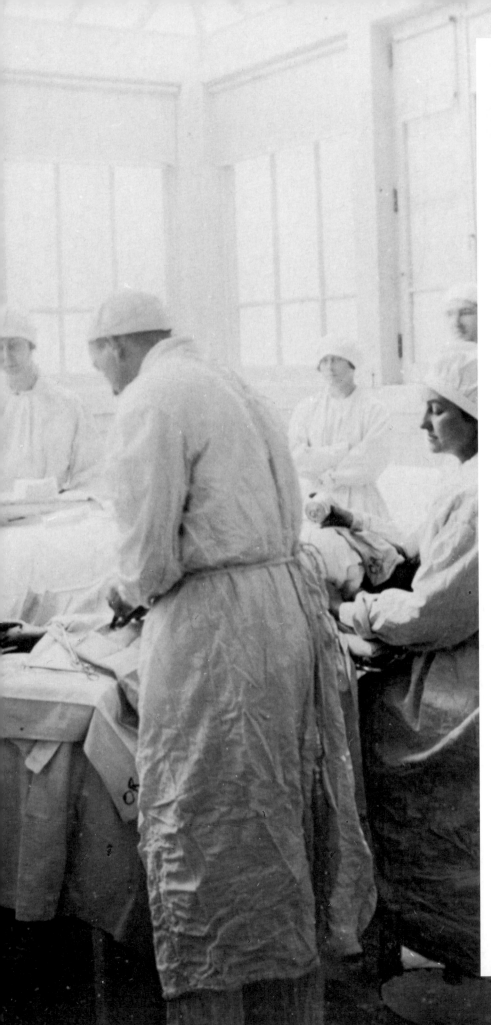

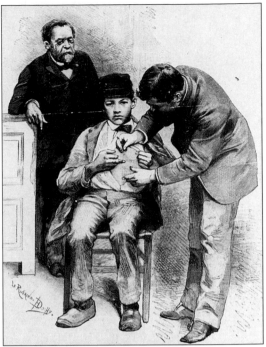

Louis Pasteur observes as an assistant vaccinates a young patient in 1885. Best known for proving that bacteria and viruses are a cause of disease, the French chemist made several contributions to medicine, including refinements to immunization.

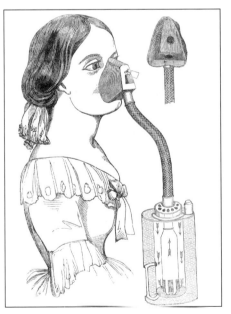

This chloroform inhaler, from an 1858 text-book, was one of the earliest devices used to administer anesthesia. Medicine entered a new era in 1846 when the medical community witnessed a demonstration of surgery without pain.

DIAGNOSTIC DEVICES

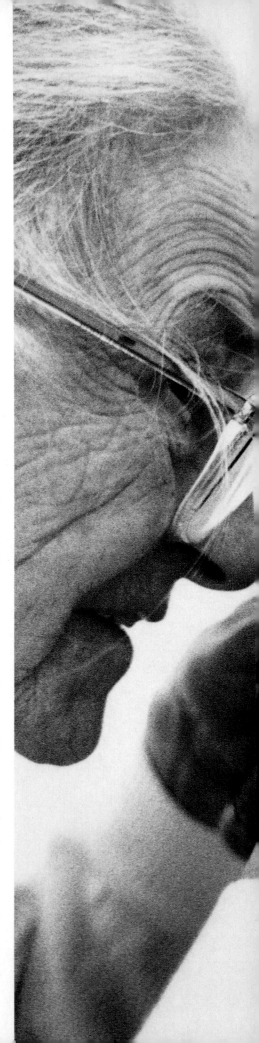

A t first, it appeared to be simple infant crankiness. But over the next few weeks, the baby's periodic whines yielded to inexplicable outbursts of crying, giving her perpetually tired eyes. Recently, her skin has become pale, her play listless; her appetite has diminished steadily over the last 10 days and today she is running a fever. Even at this stage, it may be nothing serious, but the parents prefer to consult a doctor.

Such vague ailments have challenged medicine since the days of Hippocrates. In the past, physicians relied mainly on their former experience and their senses when making a diagnosis. They prodded and squeezed, put their heads against patients' chests to hear the rush of air and the swish of fluids. They listened to the creaks of the joints and the rumble of the intestines, smelled the breath and sometimes even tasted patients' urine—sweetness was a sure sign of diabetes.

Now, physicians have at their command diagnostic tests and equipment exceeding anything known to the house-calling general practitioner of yore. Today's therapeutic armory embraces the very latest in medical technology, from biochemical assays to massive, computer-driven machines and electronic "eyes" that can peer into every nook and cranny of the body. There are systems for counting blood cells, gauging hormone levels, monitoring blood toxins and measuring the balance of essential body chemicals. Electronic sensors compile graphic records of heart function, nerve impulse and brain activity. Viewing systems for probing the body's interior go well beyond the basic X-ray camera, employing everything from sound waves to nuclear particle beams and delivering live-action photos.

Machines aside, a good diagnostician requires the skills of a master detective. Indeed, the paradigmatic Sherlock Holmes was modeled on a late-19th-Century Scottish doctor named Joseph Bell, whose celebrated diagnostic skills had impressed the young medical student and future author, Arthur Conan Doyle. Like the mythic Holmes—and real-life Bell—medical sleuths are masters of deduction, alert to little clues that conglomerate to form a total picture: Expressionless face,

---

The art of doctoring assumes not only an encyclopedic knowledge of the human body—such the form and function of this young patient's inner ear—but also keen powers of observation and deduction, as well as gentleness and compassion.

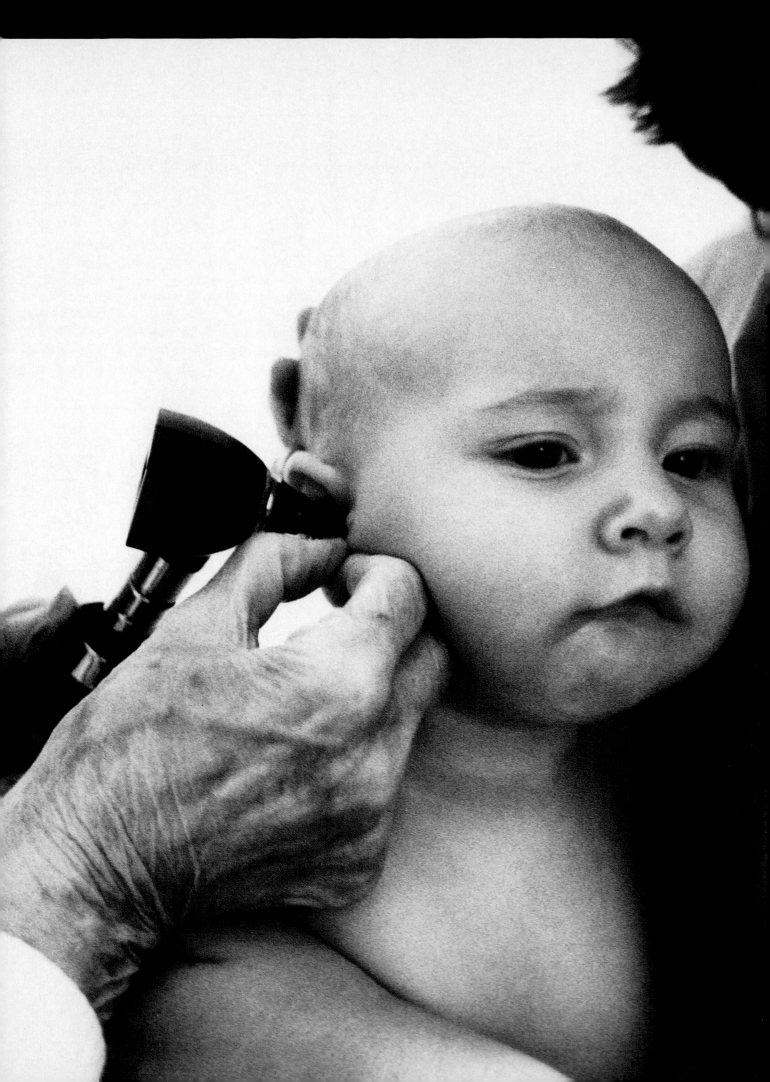

shuffling gait, hand tremors, along with the peculiar muscular stiffness known as cogwheel rigidity? Elementary, my dear Watson, the patient seems to have a neurological disorder, perhaps Parkinson's disease. A warm, moist handshake? Possibly a hint of hyperthyroidism. A "cold fish" handshake? Quite probably nervous tension. Slumped shoulders, sad expression, avoidance of eye contact: signs of depression. Fidgeting, clenched fists, leaning forward in chair: anxiety. Observant physicians start gathering evidence as to the state of their patients' health from the moment the office door opens.

Once the cause of a patient's complaint has been identified, the physician can call upon an impressive arsenal of tools and techniques to bring about a cure. Today's pharmacopeia is light years beyond the herbal elixirs used by physicians even a century ago. The development of antibiotics has revolutionized medical practice so that rheumatic fever, typhoid fever, syphilis and many other infectious diseases no longer carry a probable death sentence. The list of available antimicrobials numbers in the thousands, with new ones being added weekly. At the same time, drug researchers ply other spheres in search of new cures. They analyze the juices of tropical plants, restructure the molecules of proteins and petrochemicals, and call upon the advanced techniques of genetic engineering to synthesize everything from the insulin needed by diabetics to the interferon being used in experimental cancer treatment.

Sometimes even a preliminary diagnosis will send a patient straight to the operating table. The symptoms of heart disease, for example, can range from a burning sensation in the chest and throat, shortness of breath, or violent pains in the left shoulder and arm, to nothing more than a strange, ill-defined lethargy. After a number of preliminary tests, the doctor will have a reasonably sure idea where the problem lies. Then, to gauge its severity, he may call for an angiogram. This is an X-ray procedure that reveals the exact location and degree of blockage in the patient's coronary arteries, leading to the heart. Should the constriction appear life threatening, the patient may find himself booked into the hospital for a procedure known as balloon angioplasty. Guided by a moving X-ray image, a tiny balloon will be threaded by catheter into an artery in the patient's leg, then up to the occluded artery. At the target site, the balloon will be inflated, compressing the buildup of fatty material against the artery's walls so that blood can once again flow freely to the heart.

In emergencies, of course, physicians may have to apply treatment even before the cause of the problem has been found. Every day, thousands of people check into hospital emergency rooms, and though in most cases the reason is obvious, quite often it is not. Some have cuts and bruises apparent to the eye, others, broken bones immediately detectable by examination or X ray. Food poisoning and most common illnesses can usually be identified by a quick physical check and by questioning the patient.

But what if the patient arrives in a coma? Perhaps his heartbeat is diminished or his breathing has stopped. All effort is directed at cardiopulmonary resuscitation: the chest is massaged, a breathing tube is inserted and an injection of drugs may be given in an attempt to revive the heart. Then, when the patient has been temporarily stabilized, he can be tested for the underlying condition so that doctors can begin addressing it.

THE BODY'S SYSTEMS

Although it is most commonly perceived as a single functioning unit, the human body is, in fact, a collection of interdependent physiological teams, each with its own responsibilities and potential ailments. The two branches of the musculoskeletal system work in concert to form a mobile structure for the body. Even while that system is at rest, others remain in constant activity: The nervous and endocrine systems, for example, as well as the circulatory, respiratory, digestive and urinary systems, operate without cease to keep the body alive. When presented with symptoms of ill health, the diagnostician's first task is to assess which of the body's systems is at fault.

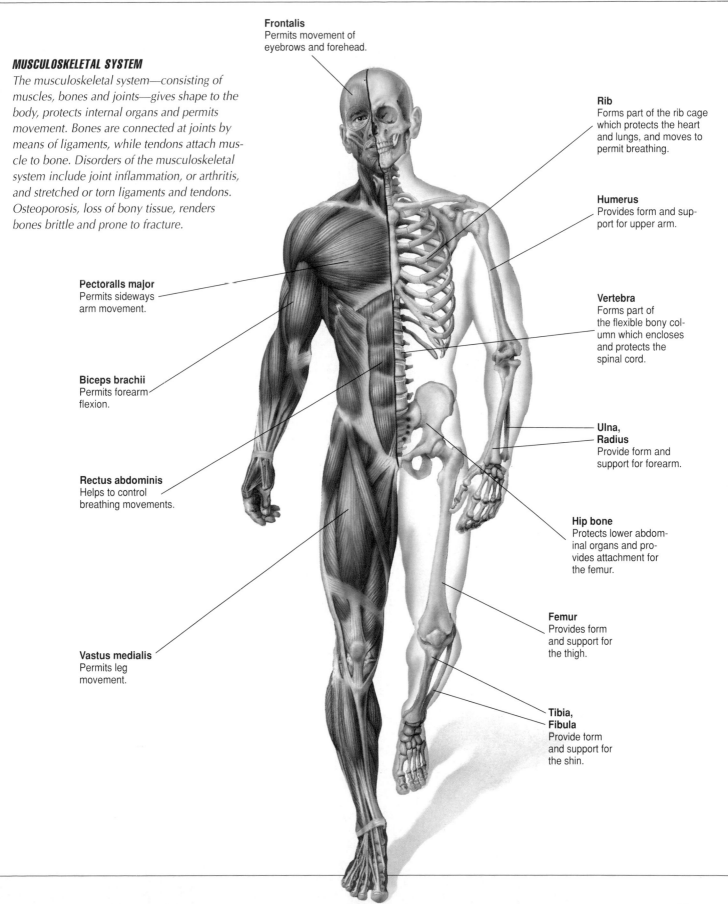

MUSCULOSKELETAL SYSTEM

The musculoskeletal system—consisting of muscles, bones and joints—gives shape to the body, protects internal organs and permits movement. Bones are connected at joints by means of ligaments, while tendons attach muscle to bone. Disorders of the musculoskeletal system include joint inflammation, or arthritis, and stretched or torn ligaments and tendons. Osteoporosis, loss of bony tissue, renders bones brittle and prone to fracture.

Frontalis
Permits movement of eyebrows and forehead.

Rib
Forms part of the rib cage which protects the heart and lungs, and moves to permit breathing.

Humerus
Provides form and support for upper arm.

Pectoralls major
Permits sideways arm movement.

Vertebra
Forms part of the flexible bony column which encloses and protects the spinal cord.

Biceps brachii
Permits forearm flexion.

**Ulna,
Radius**
Provide form and support for forearm.

Rectus abdominis
Helps to control breathing movements.

Hip bone
Protects lower abdominal organs and provides attachment for the femur.

Femur
Provides form and support for the thigh.

Vastus medialis
Permits leg movement.

**Tibia,
Fibula**
Provide form and support for the shin.

NERVOUS AND ENDOCRINE SYSTEMS

The nervous system consists of the central nervous system—brain and spinal cord—and the peripheral nervous system, composed of nerves that connect the brainstem and spinal cord with the rest of the body. Peripheral nerves convey sensory information to the brain, send signals to muscles and control automatic body activities such as intestinal contractions. Disorders include Parkinson's disease, characterized by muscle twitching, and epilepsy. The endocrine system is composed of hormone-producing glands. The pituitary gland, at the base of the brain, conducts the symphony of hormones—chemical messengers that help to maintain the status quo. Disorders include excessive or insufficient hormone production, such as hyperthyroidism due to thyroid gland overactivity, and diabetes, low insulin production.

CARDIOVASCULAR AND RESPIRATORY SYSTEMS

The cardiovascular system consists of the heart, arteries, veins and capillaries that transport blood. Blood that has passed through the lungs, to pick up oxygen and give up carbon dioxide, is sent to the heart to be pumped to a series of arteries leading to a network of capillaries. Following gaseous and chemical exchange between capillary blood and body tissue, the blood returns to the heart via a series of veins. Disorders include heart rhythm abnormalities and coronary artery disease. The process of breathing depends on the respiratory system. Inhaled air passes to the throat, through the vocal cords of the larynx and down the trachea, connected to each lung by a bronchus. Oxygen-carbon dioxide exchange occurs in the lung alveoli—tiny sponge-like air sacs. Disorders include asthma and emphysema.

NERVOUS SYSTEM

Brain
Sends, receives and interprets nervous signals.

Brainstem
Controls body's automatic functions and connects brain to spinal cord.

Cervical nerve
Forms part of a group of nerves that connect spinal cord to muscles of neck, shoulders and arms.

Thoracic nerve
Forms part of a group of nerves that connect spinal cord to muscles of the chest, abdomen and back.

Spinal cord
Transmits nervous signals between the brain and the rest of the body.

Lumbar nerve
Forms part of a group of nerves that connect spinal cord to muscles of legs.

ENDOCRINE SYSTEM

Pituitary gland
Secretes many hormones and controls the endocrine system.

Thyroid gland
Secretes thyroxine which regulates metabolism.

Adrenal glands
Secrete adrenaline, which helps to regulate blood pressure.

Pancreas
Secretes insulin and glucagon, which regulate blood sugar level.

Testes
Secrete testosterone, which is responsible for masculine characteristics. The ovaries are the female equivalent of the testes.

CARDIOVASCULAR SYSTEM

Superior vena cava
Transports blood from upper body veins to heart.

Aorta
Transports blood to other arteries.

Heart
Pumps blood throughout the body.

Inferior vena cava
Transports blood from lower body veins to heart.

RESPIRATORY SYSTEM

Larynx
Houses the vocal cords, which permit speech.

Trachea
Connects larynx and bronchi.

Lung
Houses the sponge-like air sacs that permit gas exchange.

DIGESTIVE AND URINARY SYSTEMS

The digestive system breaks down food and enables nutrient absorption. Food is chewed in the mouth, then passed to the stomach whose acid environment facilitates chemical breakdown. Enzymes secreted into the small intestine aid in digestion and nutrients are subsequently absorbed through the small intestinal wall.

Water is absorbed in the large intestine, and the dehydrated waste is expelled through the anus. Disorders of the digestive system include erosions of the stomach lining called ulcers and chronic inflammation of the large intestine or colitis. The urinary system helps to maintain a chemical balance in the body, and removes waste products from blood.

The kidneys filter blood and pass the concentrated liquid waste to the bladder, via the ureter. The waste is expelled from the body by the urethra. Disorders of this system include stones that form in the urinary tract, and cystitis (inflammation of the bladder).

DIGESTIVE SYSTEM

Mouth
Begins digestion with chewing of food and some chemical breakdown due to saliva enzymes.

Esophagus
Connects mouth to stomach.

Liver
Secretes bile, a mixture of chemicals necessary for digestion, via gallbladder into small intestine.

Stomach
Breaks down food in acidic environment.

Gallbladder
Stores bile until secretion into small intestine.

Pancreas
Secretes enzymes—for breakdown of protein, carbohydrate and fat—into small intestine.

Small intestine
Continues food digestion; site of nutrient absorption via blood capillaries.

Large intestine
Absorbs water through intestinal walls, concentrating the waste material.

Anus
Expels feces.

URINARY SYSTEM

Kidney
Filters blood to remove waste and to maintain chemical balance in body.

Ureter
Connects kidney and bladder.

Bladder
Stores urine until sufficient quantity can be voided.

Urethra
Expels urine.

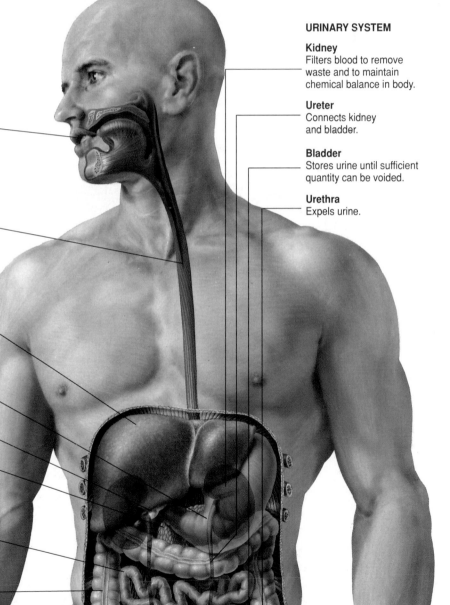

STEPS TO A DIAGNOSIS

Most ailments are, in fact, readily diagnosed by a primary care physician such as a family doctor or internist. Usually the doctor begins the medical history by having the patient describe, in his own words, the reason for his visit. The doctor asks pertinent questions to pinpoint the chronological development of symptoms, but takes care to let the patient do most of the talking. If the patient complains of pain, the physician will seek a more specific description: Is it a burning, stinging or throbbing sensation? Does it radiate to other areas? In medical parlance, the latter is known as referred pain, and it can be an important diagnostic clue. In some cases, the patient's speech itself may suggest depression or stress.

The next step is the past history, in which the physician inquires about childhood diseases, surgery, obstetrical history, hospitalizations, immunizations and allergies to any medicines. The family history is concerned with diseases for which the patient may have inherited either a predisposition—diabetes, heart disease, some types of cancer, etc.—or, as in the case of sickle-cell anemia and hemophilia, the disease itself.

A personal history gives the physician still more information about the patient, including occupation, hobbies, marital status and harmful habits such as smoking or substance abuse. The doctor will inquire about the patient's diet, sex life and recent travels, especially to areas where such diseases as malaria, amoebic dysentery and AIDS, for example, are prevalent. Some of these points may have been covered in a waiting-room questionnaire, though a direct interview reveals more about the individual. In the words of the great Canadian clinician, Sir William Osler, "Many times it is more important to know what kind of patient has the disease than it is to know what kind of disease the patient has."

Even with today's sophisticated diagnostic instrumentation, the physician begins with the simplest of data: the vital signs. Weight, temperature, pulse, respiratory rate and blood pressure remain essential indicators of health, and only slightly has technology altered their testing.

Temperature can be taken by placing the bulb of a well-shaken mercury thermometer under the patient's tongue for three minutes, or it can be obtained in less than 60 seconds by an electronic thermometer called a thermistor. A reading of 98.6°F (or 37°C) is normal, although it varies slightly from person to person and may drop a degree or two during sleep. Rectal temperatures are a full degree higher than oral readings and are less subject to errors, such as those caused by a partly open mouth. Small children and unconscious patients are best monitored by a rectal thermometer.

The pulse is usually taken by placing two or three fingers on the radial artery, at the wrist on the thumb side. The normal pulse rate in a patient at rest is 60 to 80 beats per minute. In addition to the rate, the physician assesses the regularity of the rhythm, as well as the strength of the pulse. The physician may use this occasion to count the respiratory rate, normally from 10 to 18 breaths per minute.

Blood pressure is measured with an instrument called a sphygmomanometer. Broken into two components, the readings indicate systolic pressure and diastolic pressure. Systolic—always the first figure stated—refers to the pressure within the arteries when the heart contracts to force blood through the arteries. Diastolic indicates arterial pressure when the heart relaxes. Both readings are important in deter-

ARSENAL IN A BLACK BAG

The family doctor's diagnostic arsenal fits neatly into the proverbial black bag. Today's high-tech instrumentation has not rendered obsolete such familiar tools as the stethoscope, reflex hammer, sphygmomanometer and ophthalmscope —easily converted to an otoscope.

Stethoscope
Instrument that amplifies sound, used to examine heart and lung function.

Reflex hammer
Rubber mallet, used to strike tendons in reflex testing.

Otoscope conversion parts
Attachments that transform the ophthalmoscope into an otoscope—a device for examining the outer and middle ear.

Ophthalmoscope
Viewing device for examining inside of the eye, made up of a light, mirror and magnifying lenses of different powers.

Tongue depressors
Disposable wooden sticks, used for lowering the tongue to facilitate throat examination.

Sphygmomanometer
Device for blood pressure measurement, comprised of an inflatable arm band, air bulb and pressure gauge.

mining whether a person has hypertension, the term for high blood pressure. Normal adult levels vary from person to person, fluctuating according to activity or emotional state and tending to increase with age. As a rule, anything below 140/90—systolic and diastolic, respectively—is considered normal for most adults. For the sake of accuracy, the physician will determine blood pressure in both arms—at least on the initial evaluation—and may compare readings while the patient is in different positions—sitting, standing or lying down. In some cases, the patient is asked to obtain a sphygmomanometer and take readings at home over a period of two to three weeks. As well as monitoring blood pressure during a variety of situations, this practice circumvents a phenomenon known as "white coat hypertension," where pressure rises in the doctor's office.

During the physical examination, the doctor of today still relies heavily on his senses of touch, smell, vision and hearing. Clues to internal disease display themselves prominently on the body's largest organ: the skin. Jaundiced skin may mean liver problems or a blocked bile duct due to gallstones or cancer of the pancreas.

Frozen Forensics

When medical science and the legal profession marry their investigative talents, the result is a progeny called forensics. If foul play is suspected in a death, forensic medicine often provides vital clues and evidence. And when forensics and anthropology join forces, the results are even more impressive, often providing answers to riddles that have remained unsolved for years.

One dramatic example from recent history is the 1981 investigation of an ill-fated 1845 Arctic expedition made by Sir John Franklin and 134 men in pursuit of the long-sought Northwest Passage. Franklin and his crew never returned. Almost 140 years later, Dr. Owen Beattie, a Canadian forensic anthropologist, used the tools of the 20th Century to shed light on the mystery.

Retracing the route of the original expedition, Dr. Beattie and his team painstakingly collected evidence—fragments of human bones, bits of clothing, even canned goods—all left frozen in the Arctic. The team also investigated the makeshift graves of three of the sailors; they proved to be a trove of crucial information. Following standard forensic practice, Beattie exhumed each body and carried out field autopsies, extracting valuable organ, tissue, bone and hair samples that were later analyzed in a lab.

The samples were subjected to a trace element analysis—a technique that provides insights into health and diet. Hair samples were especially interesting: The strands were long enough to show lead levels throughout the first eight months of the expedition. The results indicated acute lead poisoning; an acceptable average for lead in the body is from 5 to 14 parts per million, but some of Beattie's samples revealed lead levels exceeding 600 parts per million. The answer to the mystery lay in what was left of the expedition's canned goods. The seams of the tins were soldered with lead that had leached slowly into the food. Ironically, this expedition, equipped with everything that 19th-Century science had to offer—including canned food—paid dearly for its reliance on new technology.

Beechey Island, near the Arctic Circle, is the grave site for three members of the ill-fated Franklin expedition of 1845. Franklin's ships were icebound here.

One of the few photographs of John Torrington, a 20-year-old petty officer on the expedition, was taken almost 140 years after his death. Tissue, bone and hair samples taken from his body, preserved by the Arctic permafrost, provided forensic investigators with the answer to his cause of death.

Various rashes can be associated with specific groups of ailments, while certain telltale skin textures betray the presence of glandular disorders. The physician also checks carefully for skin cancer.

Circulatory problems may be present if the palm of the hand fails to regain its pink color after the patient clenches and unclenches a fist. Clubbing of the fingertips may be a sign of chronic lung disease or lung cancer. More mundanely, bitten fingernails suggest anxiety; unkempt nails, depression.

"Open wide and say, 'Aah.'" The doctor flattens the tongue with a disposable wooden tongue depressor, exposing the throat. A laryngeal mirror along with a head mirror and a light source illuminate the voice box to check out symptoms in cases of hoarseness. The oral cavity is examined for whitish thickened areas that precede cancer, more and more common among teenagers as snuff and chewing tobacco regain popularity. The nose is also examined, especially the mucous membrane. A light and a speculum, the tool used for holding open a body cavity, reveal inflammation.

To look into the ears, the doctor uses a combined flashlight and magnifying glass, called an otoscope. The doctor can often perceive a fluid buildup behind the tympanic membrane, or eardrum, and can spot inflammation, infection or scarring of the eardrum, indicative of a previous infection. A sophisticated pneumatic version of the instrument lets the doctor deliver tiny puffs of air against the eardrum; a normal eardrum will vibrate, while a scarred membrane or one that is tense because of fluid buildup will remain still.

The general appearance of the eyes and eyeball movement can be observed without special viewing devices. Size and equality of pupils are noted, and pupillary reaction is assessed with the aid of a small flashlight. A wall chart is used to check near and distant vision, while a pen or some hand-held object, held to the side of the eyes, tests the edges of the visual field. Glaucoma can be detected with a device called a tonometer that resembles a thin tire gauge; when placed on the eyeball, it measures the pressure of the fluid within. The ophthalmoscope—actually the same device as the otoscope, converted for eye examination—reveals early clouds of cataract and betrays such diseases as diabetes and hypertension by exposing the retina, the only place where a doctor can view the body's arteries and veins without performing surgery.

A number of senses are brought to bear in the examination of the chest. The physician observes the chest wall as the patient breathes, looking for left-right equality of expansion. Palpation—careful feeling with the hands and fingertips—reveals abnormal vibrations, called "thrills." Next, the doctor percusses over the chest, tapping a finger of one hand with the middle finger of the other hand. A nice hollow sound is normal, while dullness may indicate an abnormal

Blood pressure is tested with a sphygmomanometer, consisting of an inflatable armband and a tube of mercury indicating air pressure within the band. After the band is wrapped snugly around the upper arm, it is inflated (1). Air pressure squeezes shut the brachial artery—the main artery in the arm—at the same time forcing the mercury to the top of its column (2).

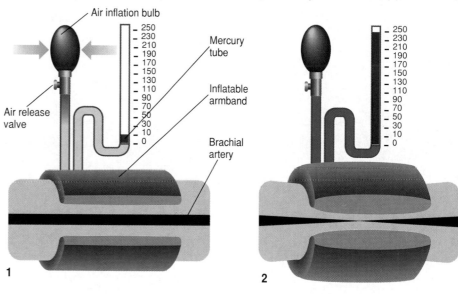

Air inflation bulb

Mercury tube

Inflatable armband

Air release valve

Brachial artery

1

2

fluid collection or—in conditions such as pneumonia—hardening of part of a lung. Too hollow—or drum-like—a sound, may indicate an abnormal amount of air in the chest cavity, or the over-distended lungs of a patient with emphysema.

The quintessential doctor's tool, the stethoscope, was born of inspired modesty. One day in 1816, French physician René Laënnec was consulted by a young woman with symptoms of heart disease. Too embarrassed to press his ear against her chest, Laënnec rolled up a newspaper and listened at a gentlemanly distance. Today's stethoscope is a more sophisticated device. Sounds from within the body are picked up by either an open bell-shaped structure or a diaphragm placed directly on the skin; rubber or plastic tubes carry the sounds to molded earpieces. Some stethoscopes are equipped with electronic amplifiers.

Indispensable in the detection of heart failure, pneumonia, asthma, emphysema and other pulmonary diseases, the stethoscope picks up unusual lung sounds whose descriptions range from the crinkle of cellophane to the whinny of a horse. Each heartbeat, as heard through the stethoscope, is characterized by a "lub-dup." This dual percussion announces the contraction of the heart's ventricles, followed by the opening and closing of the valves. Abnormal sounds, called murmurs, can indicate a damaged or diseased heart valve. The murmur's character, location and timing indicate not only which valve is faulty, but also its ailment.

The sense of touch comes to the fore again in diagnosing abdominal problems. While palpating for abnormal masses or enlargement of organs such as the liver or spleen, the doctor also watches for involuntary flinching that indicates sore spots. The abdomen is then percussed similarly to the chest. A dull sound from the intestine indicates fluid; a drum-like sound in the bowel may point to an intestinal obstruction. Suspicions of intestinal blockage can be confirmed with the stethoscope, which normally reports discrete rushing sounds; a silent abdomen can mean peritonitis—the inflammation of the abdominal cavity—or a similar condition in which the bowel is temporarily paralyzed.

The nervous system is tested by examining motor and sensory functions. Muscle contraction is assessed in all parts of the body and reflexes are tested with a rubber mallet. Pain sensation is checked by pricking the skin with a sterile needle; touch, by passing a wisp of cotton across the skin.

Naturally, the exam varies according to gender. If the patient is female, the physician will palpate the breasts for unusual lumps or thickening and will examine under the armpits for enlarged lymph glands—a possible indicator of the spread of cancer. As well, he will perform a pelvic examination, inspecting the external genitalia, the vagina and the cervix. A Pap smear, a sample of cervical cells, is taken and sent for laboratory analysis. The doctor also palpates the cervix and the internal genitalia, including the uterus, Fallopian tubes and ovaries, in search

Next, the artery is monitored with a stethoscope while air is slowly released from the valve, loosening the band. As the armband is loosened, a loud "boom" punctuates the first spurt of blood through the artery; at this instant the level on the mercury column is recorded as systolic pressure (3). Diastolic pressure—the lower of the two values—is recorded when the blood begins to flow silently (4).

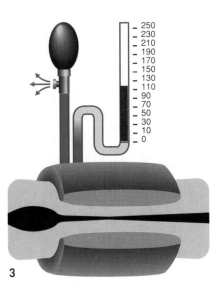

3

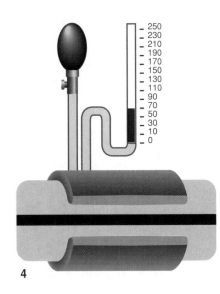

4

of enlargement or tumors. Finally, a digital examination of the rectum detects most rectal cancers.

In the male, the penis, testes, prostate gland and lymph nodes are carefully examined. Knots or masses in the testes may indicate cancer of the testicle—most frequently a young man's disease. A rectal exam is always included, not only to rule out rectal tumors, but also to assess the prostate for enlargement or cancer. Few parts of the physical are more important to a man middle-aged or older.

INNER VISION

If an initial checkup is inconclusive, or raises suspicions of a particular ailment, the physician may employ more advanced diagnostic tools. Incorporating computer technology and miniaturized electronics, these devices not only make bodily measurements with a detail and precision exceeding those of mechanical implements, but also record data over time. As well, they display anatomical and physiological data visually, either on a TV monitor or, in some cases, on a computer printout.

The electrocardiograph (ECG or EKG) is an adjunct to the sphygmomanometer and stethoscope in showing how the heart ticks. Like all muscular movement, each of the heart's contractions is stimulated by a tiny electrical current. Even though they are three thousand times weaker than currents in a pocket flashlight, these surges can be detected by sensors placed on the skin of the chest. Voltage changes are portrayed as jagged lines, either on a moving strip of paper—an electrocardiogram—or on the screen of an electrocardiograph. A characteristic three-peaked pattern occurs during every contraction. These peaks identify aberrations such as palpitations or arrhythmias—irregular rhythms—even pinpointing their source. Absence of the first peak, for example, indicates either malfunctioning chambers or a problem in the sinus node—the heart's master timekeeper.

Typically when an ECG is taken, 10 electrodes are attached with an electrically conductive gel—one on each of the arms and legs, six on the chest. ECG readings usually are taken during a so-called stress test; patients run on a motorized treadmill or pedal a stationary bicycle. Stress tests are often used to determine safe exercise levels for middle-aged and heart-attack patients. In suspected cases of rhythm disturbances or chest pain, the doctor might recommend an ambulatory electrocardiogram, which monitors the heart for 24 hours or more while the patient continues normal daily activities—working, eating, sleeping, even having sex. A small portable ECG called a Holter monitor is worn at the waist or hung from a shoulder strap, with up to five leads attached to the chest. The recording tape, chronicling as many as 100,000 heartbeats, can then be thoroughly analyzed by computer.

Similar signal-monitoring is used to study the brain, where a maelstrom of electrical activity occurs. Recorded by an instrument called an electroencephalograph (EEG), these electrical fluctuations appear, either on screen or on paper, as wavy

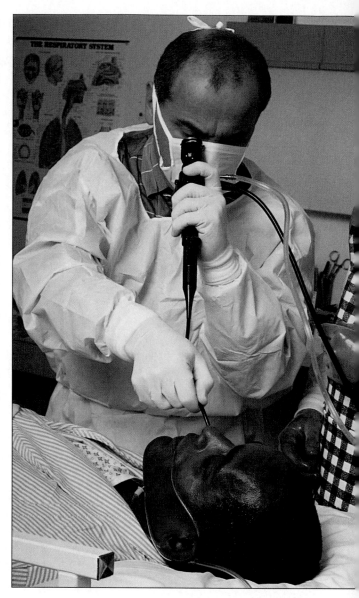

Peering down a flexible viewing device called a bronchoscope, the physician examines branches of the bronchial tree. Fiber-optic cables transmit light to the viewing site, while other cables carry an image to the doctor's eye. The instrument also is equipped with a pinching mechanism for snipping off tissue samples for biopsies, as well as a water-supply line to flush away resultant blood.

lines of varying frequency and shape. A readout of the recorded brainwaves is called an electroencephalogram.

Like the ECG, the EEG uses electrodes on the skin, but the brain's electrical signals are a thousand-fold weaker than the heart's and are much more numerous and scattered. For this procedure, up to 22 electrodes are distributed over the scalp. Chaotic as the resulting rows of squiggles may appear, EEGs can be used to elucidate suspected brain-related disorders ranging from epilepsy to insomnia.

Yet another application of the same basic principle is the electromyograph, or EMG. Muscle function depends on similar electrical signals, as the 18th-Century Italian researcher Luigi Galvani proved when he electroshocked the legs of a frog into flexing. Failure in the telegraph system uniting motor nerve cells can often be detected by using electromyography: One electrode is fixed to the surface of the skin and the other, an ultrafine needle, is inserted directly into the muscle; as the patient tries to flex the muscle, the machine measures the electric charge between the two sensors.

An entirely different method of peering inside the body updates a technology dating to the early 19th Century. In those days, doctors looked into orifices by inserting a rigid hollow tube, called an endoscope, and squinting down it under flickering candlelight. Today's endoscopes utilize fiber-optics. This amazing technology uses flexible strands of the purest glass no thicker than a hair, but whose walls deflect beams of light like balls caroming through the gates of a pinball machine. Diagnostic endoscopes contain two bundles of fiberglass tubing: One carries light into the body; the other sends an image of the organ to the doctor's eye, a camera lens or the screen of a video monitor. Some endoscopic designs can even collect tissue samples.

To examine the lungs, for example, the physician threads the fiber-optic tube into the respiratory tract via the nose or mouth, down the bronchial tubes—hence the name of the practice, bronchoscopy—and into the smaller air passages of the lungs. As much as three feet of tubing may be snaked into the body. From the instrument's controlling end, the doctor looks for signs of pulmonary disease, and may also clear away obstructing mucus or take biopsy samples for lab analysis.

The endoscope is also used to explore the digestive tract. Although the same instrument travels to different regions of the upper tract, each examination has its own name: If the specially adapted instrument is pushed down into the esophagus, the procedure is called esophagoscopy; into the stomach, gastroscopy; and as far as the top of the duodenum, or small intestine, duodenoscopy. The large intestine, approached through the rectum, is a common target of endoscopy in North America, where cancer of the colon rates second only to lung cancer. During a colonoscopy, the physician looks for malignancies and snips away polyps—small growths that might prove cancerous.

Cystoscopy explores the urinary tract, including the interior of the bladder, while laparoscopy permits a view of the liver, spleen and pancreas, as well as the ovaries. In the latter case, gas is used to inflate the abdominal cavity, creating a viewing space. Since it does not snake through a natural passageway, the laparoscope is a rigid instrument; its introduction into the abdomen requires a small incision in or just above the navel.

With bronchoscopy, where a fiber-optic tube is threaded into the bronchial tubes through the mouth and throat, the diagnostician is able to see into the deepest recesses of the lungs. This patient's bronchial tubes are a healthy pink, glistening under fiber-optic light.

DIGITAL DIAGNOSIS

A middle-aged woman, who has been experiencing lower back pain for the last month, describes the symptoms to her doctor. Although the pain is acutely real to her, its cause is much less apparent to her physician: The symptoms could be the physical manifestation of a number of diseases, but the doctor must correctly diagnose the disease so that proper treatment can begin.

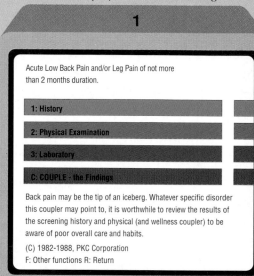

1

Acute Low Back Pain and/or Leg Pain of not more than 2 months duration.

1: History

2: Physical Examination

3: Laboratory

C: COUPLE - the Findings

Back pain may be the tip of an iceberg. Whatever specific disorder this coupler may point to, it is worthwhile to review the results of the screening history and physical (and wellness coupler) to be aware of poor overall care and habits.

(C) 1982-1988, PKC Corporation
F: Other functions R: Return

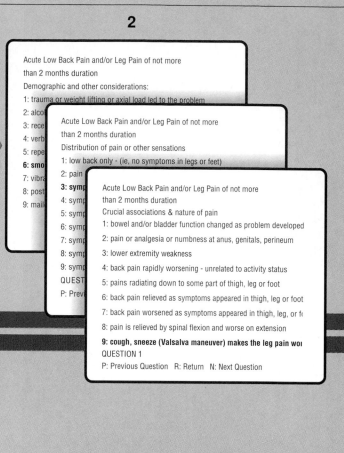

2

Acute Low Back Pain and/or Leg Pain of not more than 2 months duration
Demographic and other considerations:
1: trauma or weight lifting or axial load led to the problem
2: alco
3: rece
4: verb
5: repe
6: smo
7: vibra
8: post
9: mail

Acute Low Back Pain and/or Leg Pain of not more than 2 months duration
Distribution of pain or other sensations
1: low back only - (ie, no symptoms in legs or feet)
2: pain
3: symp
4: symp
5: symp
6: symp
7: symp
8: symp
9: symp
QUEST
P: Previ

Acute Low Back Pain and/or Leg Pain of not more than 2 months duration
Crucial associations & nature of pain
1: bowel and/or bladder function changed as problem developed
2: pain or analgesia or numbness at anus, genitals, perineum
3: lower extremity weakness
4: back pain rapidly worsening - unrelated to activity status
5: pains radiating down to some part of thigh, leg or foot
6: back pain relieved as symptoms appeared in thigh, leg or foot
7: back pain worsened as symptoms appeared in thigh, leg, or fo
8: pain is relieved by spinal flexion and worse on extension
9: cough, sneeze (Valsalva maneuver) makes the leg pain wor
QUESTION 1
P: Previous Question   R: Return   N: Next Question

3

Acute Low Back Pain and/or Leg Pain of not more than 2 months duration
Muscle examination for weakness:
1: weak resisted flexion at knee
2: wea
3: limit
4: wea
5: wea
6: wea
7: foot
8: wea
9: pain
QUEST
P: Prev

Acute Low Back Pain and/or Leg Pain of not more than 2 months duration
Straight leg raising tests:
1: radiating pain on raising straight leg more than 35 degrees
2: pain on raising straight leg less than 30 degrees - bilateral
3: straight leg raising painful/limited only when int rotated
4: active resistance to straight leg raising
5: positive crossed straight leg raising test
6: pain on passive flexion of knee when prone (heel to buttock)
QUESTION 8
P: Previous Question   R: Return   N: Next Question

Rather than relying on his memory to sort through the many possible causes of back pain, the doctor calls upon an online medical expert—a software program designed to help physicians with difficult diagnostic choices. These programs, like the one displayed on the computer screens above and at right, prompt the physician to provide information about the patient's medical history, physical examination and the results of any lab tests. Some programs use a technique that mimics human reasoning. The program follows a logic tree of branching options: The presence of a particular symptom prompts one series of questions; its absence elicits a different set of queries. Other programs not only supply diagnoses based on information elicited from the doctor and patient, but also let them know when more information—additional lab tests, perhaps—is required.

Though computers will never replace the flesh-and-blood diagnostician, they do facilitate a quick and accurate diagnosis. And constant updating of diagnostic software has the potential to extend the latest expert knowledge from major medical research centers to even the most remote rural medical practice.

5

Coupler: Acute Low Back Pain and/or Leg Pain or not more
than 2 months duration.
***> OBSERVED FINDINGS
Symptoms from buttock -> outer thigh -> leg -> dorsal foot -> big toe
numbness and/or paresthesiae in lower extrem - esp. leg/foot
tenderness over the sciatic notch
lumbosacral area pain after prolonged posture or activity
cough, sneeze (Valsalva maneuver) makes the leg pain worse
radiating pain on raising straight leg more than 35 degrees
Pain on passive flexion of the knee when prone (heel to buttock) may
help to localize the site of pain. Although not specific for any particular lesion, some consider it more reliable to rule out a disk than
straight leg raising.
[Refs: 1078]
weak resisted dorsiflexion of the foot
5-10 year history of episodic low back pain
smoking
sedimentation rate is elevated

4

Acute Low Back Pain and/or Leg Pain of not more
than 2 months duration
Relevant laboratory findings:
1: hematuria (blood in the urine)
2: elevated sedimentation rate
3: albuminuria
4: serology has been positive in the past and/or positive now
5: hypercalcemia
QUESTION 11
P: Previous Question   R; Return   N: Next Question

- Possible Cases	Obs/Tot	PrX	Rx
1: Osteomyelitis, Diskitis or Epidural Abscess.	1:5		
2. Disc displacement (Herniated nuc. pulposus)	3:10		
3. Tabes	1:6		
4: Pyriformis syndrome	1:7		
5: RISK FACTORS FOR A DISK DISORDER	2:3		
6: RISK FACTORS FOR LUMBAGO	1:5		
7: 4th lumbar root lesion	2:2		
8: 5th lumbar root lesion	1:5		
O: Display Cause information			
D: Change display mode - [normal]-			

P: Print Results   F: Findings   R : Return

SYMPTOM SOFTWARE

*These computer screens illustrate the different
steps a medical software program takes to pinpoint a diagnosis. To select one of the four
main categories of the program, displayed on
the main menu (1), the doctor types in the corresponding number. Questions about the history of the back pain appear on the screen (2),
and the doctor tags all the relevant responses.
The software program computes the information provided by the history-taking and presents
a series of questions and responses that concern the physical condition of the patient.
Working through the list, the doctor highlights
all the appropriate responses (3). The program
runs through all the relevant laboratory tests
and the doctor responds accordingly (4). If the
doctor has not yet requested the test, the program acts as a reminder to do so. The findings
from each category are combined (5), and the
program compares the number of observed
findings with the total number of findings associated with this ailment. The program next provides a list of diagnostic options appropriate to
this patient.*

Suggested Cause: Tabes
--Findings Present--
   numbness and/or paresthesiae in lower extrem-- esp. leg/foot
--Findings Not Present--
syphilis
patellar re
ankle re
gait is b
absent p

In tabes
percussi
the body
lumbar p
pathic jo
pain, ev

Suggested Cause: Osteomyelitis, Diskitis or Epidural Abscess
- Findings Present -
sedimentation rate is elevated .....
- Findings Not Present -
bowel an
percussi
lumbar p
An EPID
tion and
can be ra
Infection
 disk or
coccus i
when si..
Diskitis

Suggested Cause: Disc displacement (Herniated nuc. pulposus)
- Findings Present -
numbness and/or paresthesiae in lower extrem - esp;. leg/foot radiating pain on raising straight leg more than 35 degrees. cough,
sneeze (Valsalva maneuver) makes the leg pain worse
- Findings Not Present -
weakness in lower extremity(s)
relief of the back pain with the onset of the leg pain
pains radiating down to some part of thigh or leg or foot
patellar reflex depressed or absent
positive crossed straight leg raising test
ankle reflex - diminished or absent
weak resisted extension of the great toe
The onset of disc pain may be sudden/sharp or insidious. Tearing or
snapping sensations may occur. Back pain may stop as leg pain
appears. A list may be to or away from side of lesion (type of pro-

In one of the most revolutionary breakthroughs of the century, fiber-optic instruments are being applied in examining fetuses in the womb, in order to track growth and to identify any deformities or abnormalities.

Of course the most familiar device for "seeing" into the body is still the X ray. Of the same family as ordinary sunlight, X rays nevertheless pack much more energy, enabling them to penetrate human flesh. Wilhelm Roentgen, the German physicist who stumbled upon the then-unknown rays in 1895, gave the world an image that revolutionized medicine: the bones of his wife's hand with her wedding band floating around her ring finger.

Roentgen had put a photographic plate directly under her hand and the X-ray tube above it. Since X-ray radiation passes more easily through soft tissue than through bone, and is blocked entirely by metal, more radiation fell on the film under the fleshy areas, making them appear dark; less fell in the area of the bones, leaving them light; and none at all touched the film under the gold ring, producing a silhouette.

Newspapers around the world printed the remarkable black-and-white image, and in the ensuing fad for X-raying, couples had pictures taken of their hands—or rather bones—lovingly clasped. Doctors immediately recognized the potential for locating fractures, finding swallowed objects and identifying such problems as kidney or gallstones, cysts and tumors.

Today, X rays are most frequently used to diagnose dental cavities, lung and breast cancer. Many doctors recommend that women have a breast X ray, called a mammogram, sometime between the ages of 35 and 40. Women between 40 and 50 are advised to have the test every two years, followed by an annual X ray from then on.

For bodily organs that do not show up as well in X rays, contrasting agents can either increase or diminish the opacity of the tissue. Barium sulfate, a chalky substance ingested by patients before gastrointestinal X rays, coats the stomach and intestinal walls. A dye, introduced by catheter through the nose, can reveal the myriad passageways of the bronchial tree. Arteries and veins are made visible by radiopaque iodine solutions. The doctor threads a needle-thin catheter through a blood vessel to the target site while watching its slow progress on a fluoroscope. The exacting procedure, called angiography, can be used to examine deeply seated arteries such as the aorta or the coronary arteries and even can show the blood struggling past obstacles.

As far back as the 1930s, doctors realized that if two X rays were taken—one just before the injection of a contrast dye, then another immediately after—the two could be used to create a third, superior, image. The clutter of background bones and tissue seen in the first image would be subtracted from the second, thus leaving only the dyed tissue visible for study. In today's version of this digital subtraction angiography—DSA—a computer does the subtraction electronically, making a permanent filmed record while images are displayed on a video screen. The computer also can substitute colors for an X ray's normal gray tones, making the reading of such images much easier.

Computers perform even more spectacularly in CT, or computed tomography, a sectional representation. CT scans cut through overlying bone, muscles and tissue like a magician's saw, compiling multiple images into a single cross-sectional

COMPUTED TOMOGRAPHY

Taking X-ray technology one step further, the CT scan opened a new era of body imaging. By combining revolving X rays with a computer, CT scans produce *in vivo* anatomical "slices" of soft tissue. For the first time, many anatomical abnormalities could be identified without cutting the flesh.

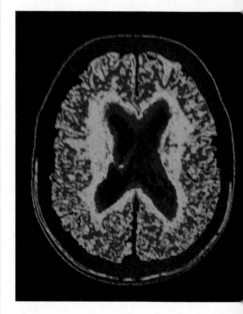

This CT brain image, color-enhanced by computer, reveals a healthy anatomical uniformity. Although CT scanning is applied to virtually all parts of the body, it is frequently used to plumb the hidden depths of the brain, prominently displaying abnormalities such as tumors or lesions.

MAPPING THE BODY'S SOFT TISSUE

In scanning a patient's head, the revolving X-ray tube of the computed tomography, or CT, machine projects a beam that passes through the head at hundreds of different angles. A detector opposite the X-ray tube measures the remaining force of each ray after it has passed through tissues. The degree of X-ray absorption is relative to the density of the tissue and provides data that a computer then translates into a visual "slice." Colored laser beams help to center the part of the body being scanned. The precise aim of CT enables cross-sectional images at any depth or angle desired. For successive slices, a technician adjusts the motorized table on which the patient rests within the doughnut hole of the scanner.

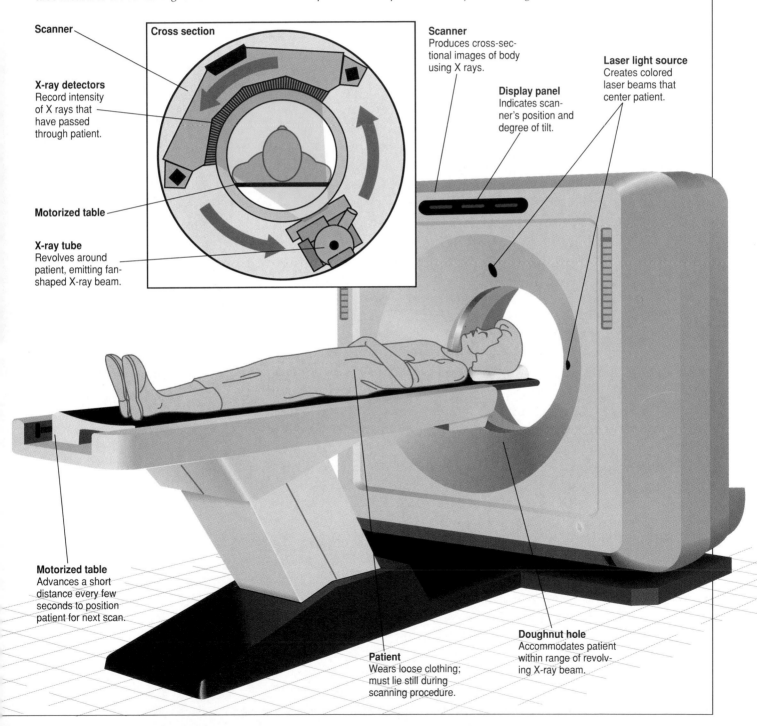

Scanner

Cross section

X-ray detectors
Record intensity of X rays that have passed through patient.

Motorized table

X-ray tube
Revolves around patient, emitting fan-shaped X-ray beam.

Scanner
Produces cross-sectional images of body using X rays.

Display panel
Indicates scanner's position and degree of tilt.

Laser light source
Creates colored laser beams that center patient.

Motorized table
Advances a short distance every few seconds to position patient for next scan.

Patient
Wears loose clothing; must lie still during scanning procedure.

Doughnut hole
Accommodates patient within range of revolving X-ray beam.

"slice." Some newer scanners go one step further, turning successive slices into three-dimensional images that can be rotated on the computer screen.

Yet, superb as it may be, X-ray radiation is ionizing, creating potentially harmful electrical charges in cells. While the amount of radiation used in CT scanning and other forms of X-raying is extremely small nowadays, the doses build up with each exposure. Fortunately, medicine's satchel of imaging tricks contains some non-ionizing alternatives. One of these is sonography, or ultrasound—similar to the echolocation used by bats, porpoises and submarines to pinpoint unseen objects by timing how long it takes sounds to bounce back from them.

An ultrasound examination utilizes a small device known as a transducer, capable of both generating and receiving high-frequency sounds beyond the range of the human ear. The strength and timing of sound waves reflecting off tissue are directly proportional to the tissue's density and distance. The transducer converts the echoes into electrical pulses, which are then assembled by a computer into a video image. Such sonograms show the location, size, shape and texture of organs, bones, blood vessels or unusual growths. Watery cysts, tumors and other soft tissue may elude X rays, but will not be overlooked by ultrasound.

Working similarly to a traffic cop's radar gun, an ultrasound technique called echocardiography can detect direction and velocity of blood flow. This technique relies on the Doppler effect: the familiar shift in frequency that occurs when a sound, for example a siren, rises in pitch as its source moves toward a listener, or falls in pitch while the source moves away. In this case the moving sound source is an echoing river of blood cells. Echocardiography has become a reliable tool in diagnosing heart conditions.

Another nonionizing scanning method, magnetic resonance imaging, or MRI, has created even more of a sensation. Like X ray, MRI is based on a discovery in the physics lab: When the nuclei of hydrogen atoms—single protons, all spinning randomly—are caught suddenly in a strong magnetic field, they tend to line up like so many compass needles. If the protons are then hit with a short, precisely tuned burst of radio waves, they will momentarily flip around. Then, in the process of returning to their original orientation, they resound with a brief radio signal of their own. The intensity of this emission reflects the number of protons in a particular "slice" of matter.

The human body's high water content gives it more atoms of hydrogen than of any other element. This makes it ideal for MRI. Slid into a contraption vaguely resembling a CT scanner, the patient is subjected to a powerful magnetic field, thousands of times stronger than the Earth's—yet as far as anyone can tell, entirely harmless to tissue. Rapidly switching the magnetic field's direction, the machine follows each change with a carefully timed radio pulse, producing a succession of bizarre, disembodied noises: a cranky old lawnmower, a car scraping bottom on a railroad track, a landing jet. As the patient's hydrogen molecules respond with radio signals of their own, the machine's radio antenna samples the signals along a particular plane of interest—say, of the brain—and a computer assembles them into a detailed cross section.

Beyond the absence of ionizing radiation, MRI's main attraction is the clarity of its imagery, which in important respects exceeds that of X-ray techniques. MRI is especially adept at detecting extremely small tumors, revealing the subtleties

MAGNETIC RESONANCE IMAGING

The technology known as MRI exploits the electromagnetic properties of hydrogen molecules to create refined anatomical images. The noninvasive technique is especially useful in the diagnosis of brain disease, although its high resolution and sharp aim are also invaluable in evaluating blood flow and in spotting tumors anywhere in the body.

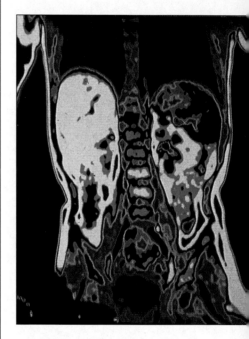

Color enhancement of MRI images, such as this one of a healthy adult's abdomen, distinguishes different types of soft tissue. Like computed tomography, MRI scans permit the diagnostician to detect abnormalities in tissue without exploratory surgery.

CREATING REFINED ANATOMICAL IMAGES

Within the metallic cocoon of an MRI scanner, the patient is surrounded by four electromagnetic coils and the components of a transceiver—a device that both sends and receives radio signals. Acting in tandem with the electromagnets, the transceiver emits radio signals that elicit corresponding signals from the body's hydrogen protons (diagrams 1 to 4, below). A computer analyzes the protons' signals and creates a detailed image of the body's soft tissue.

Scanner
Uses electromagnets and radio signals to produce cross-sectional images.

Y coil
Creates varying magnetic field from top to bottom across scanning tube.

Z coil
Creates varying magnetic field from head to toe within scanning tube.

Transceiver
Sends radio signals to protons and receives signals from them.

X coil
Creates varying magnetic field from left to right across scanning tube.

Main coil
Surrounds patient with uniform magnetic field.

Patient
Wears loose clothing; must empty pockets of metallic objects that could prove harmful if moved by magnetic force.

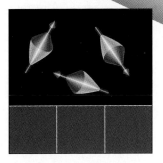

1. Hydrogen protons, positively charged particles in the hydrogen molecule's nucleus, normally spin in random directions.

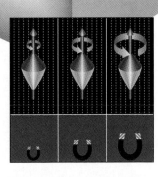

2. Protons wobble in alignment with magnetic fields of varying intensity; frequency of wobble is proportionate to strength of individual magnetic field.

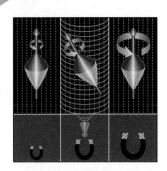

3. A brief radio signal, whose soundwave frequency equals the frequency of wobble of certain protons, knocks those protons out of alignment.

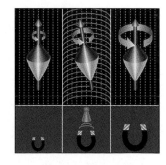

4. When radio signal ceases, protons snap back into alignment with magnetic field, emitting a radio signal of their own that announces the presence of a specific tissue.

between the brain's gray and white matter, pinpointing blockages in blood vessels or damage to vertebral disks. Some doctors are using it to examine injured knees. Neurologists in particular like it because it can expose trouble spots in the brain, such as faint areas of inflammation.

Medical researchers are experimenting with even more powerful magnets to stimulate responses from protons other than those of hydrogen. Known as magnetic resonance spectroscopy, this kindred technique permits the identification and measurement of key bodily chemicals without biopsies or biochemical tests—just by using magnetism and radio waves. Such *in vivo* metabolic testing is already being tried: Doctors are using MRS to monitor chemotherapy in cancer patients by looking for subtle chemical changes soon after administering a drug, rather than waiting weeks for a tumor to regress—or grow.

While magnetic resonance cajoles the body's own atoms into revealing something about themselves, nuclear medicine does the opposite: It supplies the body with foreign atoms that do the talking. The telltale atoms, called radioisotopes, are chemically indistinguishable from other atoms that may be found in the body—a radioisotope of oxygen, for example, reacts with other atoms as though it were standard oxygen. What does distinguish radioisotopes are their nuclei. Inherently unstable, they break apart, resulting in small bursts of energy called photons. Gamma rays released during these tiny radiant explosions can be detected by special crystals.

Injected, inhaled or swallowed, solutions of such "tagged" atoms can easily be traced with radiation detectors as they follow the body's metabolic pathways to their logical destination. The thyroid, for example, relies heavily on iodine. So, to check the functioning of a patient's thyroid, doctors use iodine solutions tagged with a small amount of radioactive isotope. When this labeled material enters the thyroid, the iodine concentration can readily be ascertained by measuring the isotope's emissions. Similarly, cardiologists frequently inject the radioisotope thallium-201 to study blood flow in the coronary arteries, sometimes immediately following the administration of a stress test.

Since the 1960s, large stationary gamma-ray cameras have been available to pick up radiation from the body and create pictures on film of the organs where the tagged atoms concentrate. While the images are not very good at revealing anatomical detail, they excel at providing clues to physiological processes, such as the loss of calcium in the bones, the spread of a tumor and the flow of blood in the heart and coronary arteries.

The first gamma-ray cameras produced only single-plane views, like old-fashioned X rays. Nowadays it is possible to take photographs at different angles in one examining session, or even to produce a moving picture. One type of machine uses gamma-ray cameras mounted on movable arms that rotate completely around the patient; a computer processes this collected data into a cross-sectional video image. Because they detect one photon at a time, such machines are called single photon emission computed tomography scanners (SPECT).

Another important type of machine uses special radioisotopes called positron emitters, which simultaneously give off two photons in opposite directions. Many of these positron emitters are chemically indistinguishable from the elements that are abundant in the body, such as carbon, nitrogen, fluorine and oxygen. To detect

POSITRON EMISSION TOMOGRAPHY

Leading the field of health technology called nuclear medicine, PET imaging shows the body's metabolism in action. Like CT and MRI, PET is a boon to the diagnosis of brain malfunctions. Unlike the other two, which provide static anatomical images, PET contributes a moving picture of chemical processes.

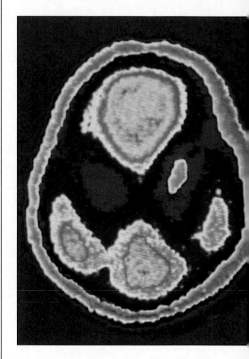

This PET scan of a normal brain displays a healthy configuration of electrochemical activity—its blue seas reflect tranquility, while its yellow and red islands show intracellular communication. Disorders such as Alzheimer's disease are characterized by gaping black holes, the result of neuronal death.

TRACKING THE BODY'S CHEMICALS

PET monitors the body's consumption of nutrients or other substances such as drugs by tracking short-lived radioactive particles in the blood. A radioactive "tag" can trace the route of glucose, for exam-

ple, to fuel-hungry cells in the brain. When the particles disintegrate, two gamma rays dart in opposite directions, striking a ring of detectors around the patient's head (inset). The radiant energy of the

rays causes crystals in the detectors to emit light, which is subsequently amplified by photomultiplier tubes. A computer deduces the rays' source, then translates the data into an image.

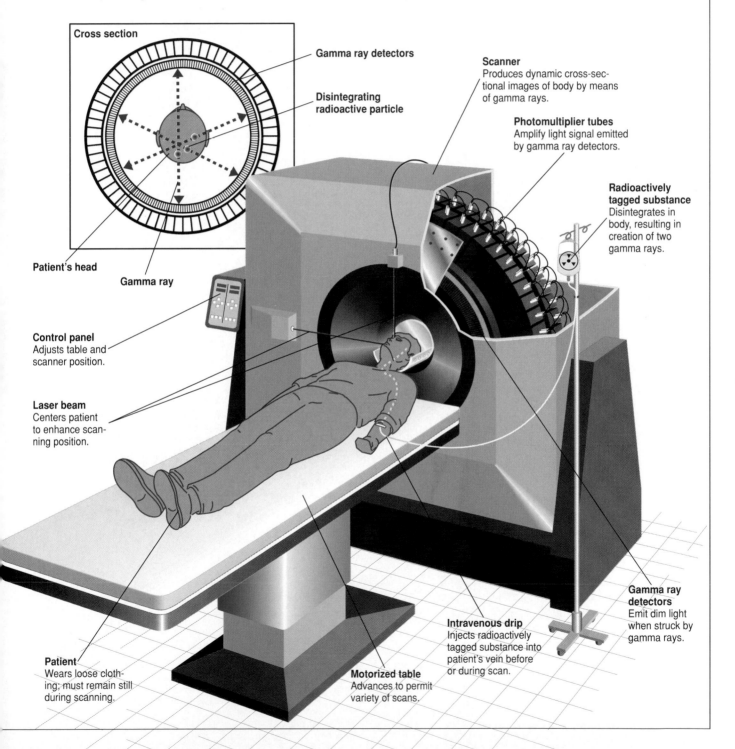

Cross section

Gamma ray detectors

Disintegrating radioactive particle

Patient's head

Gamma ray

Control panel
Adjusts table and scanner position.

Laser beam
Centers patient to enhance scanning position.

Patient
Wears loose clothing; must remain still during scanning.

Scanner
Produces dynamic cross-sectional images of body by means of gamma rays.

Photomultiplier tubes
Amplify light signal emitted by gamma ray detectors.

Radioactively tagged substance
Disintegrates in body, resulting in creation of two gamma rays.

Gamma ray detectors
Emit dim light when struck by gamma rays.

Intravenous drip
Injects radioactively tagged substance into patient's vein before or during scan.

Motorized table
Advances to permit variety of scans.

Germ Geography

When a group of people in the same geographical area simultaneously develop the same disease, it is time to call in the epidemiologist. This medical detective interviews patients, studies specimens in the lab, prepares precise maps of where the cases occurred and, finally, analyzes the resultant data.

Frequently epidemiologists uncover entirely new diseases, caused by a host of factors that might include a new toxic industrial pollutant or the emergence of a virus that previously infected only animals.

In the summer of 1975, a group of 39 children in Old Lyme, Connecticut, developed the symptoms of rheumatoid arthritis. This outbreak was extremely suspicious, because the disease is rare in children and not known to be infectious. After questioning the families, an epidemiologist noted that all of the victims lived near the woods and that their symptoms were most apparent in summer or fall. Aware that insects are abundant in the woods, the investigator suggested that insect transmission was spreading the disease.

A breakthrough came when one of the patients saved a tick that had bitten him prior to the onset of symptoms. The tick was soon identified as a new species, *Ixodes dammini*, yet it was a full six years after the Old Lyme outbreak that a tick expert in Montana discovered that the tick harbored a corkscrew-shaped bacterium, the causative agent of Lyme disease.

Scientists had already noted that tick populations had increased dramatically in the northeastern U.S., due in part to exploding populations of deer—on which ticks feed —and the regrowth of their forest habitats. The ticks had started to bite humans, thus transmitting the disease-causing bacterium. Fortunately, it is easily treated with antibiotics.

While the geographic spread of disease is a concern with epidemics due to an infectious agent such as Lyme disease and AIDS breakouts of ailments due to regional contamination, such as the cases cited in Spain and Japan *(opposite)*, are comparatively easier to contain.

Old Lyme, United States
In September 1975, the outbreak of 39 cases of childhood arthritis raised alarm. The culprit was later identified as Lyme disease, transmitted by a tick-borne bacterium, *Borrelia burgdorferi.*

Los Angeles, United States
In June 1981, a rare form of pneumonia was described in five otherwise healthy men. These cases led to an investigation into this new disease, later called AIDS (Acquired Immune Deficiency Syndrome), caused by HIV (Human Immunodeficiency Virus).

Philadelphia, United States
In July 1976, acute lung failure resulted in the death of 12 members of the American Legion following a convention. This new ailment, later called Legionnaire's disease, resulted from the spread of the bacterium, *Legionella pneumophila*, via the convention hotel's faulty air conditioning system.

Mapping the incidence of disease outbreak sometimes reveals clusters of outbreaks. This geographical information often provides epidemiologists —medical specialists who track down the causes of disease—with vital clues to the nature of the problem.

Minamata Bay, Japan
In August 1956, unusual central nervous system disorders were reported in 52 residents. Mercury poisoning, due to local industrial waste, was later identified as the cause of this illness.

Ebola River, Zaire
In August 1976, more than 200 people developed a fatal disease characterized by high fever and severe hepatitis. The virus responsible for this blood-borne disease, later called Ebola disease, also was named after the Zairian river near whose banks it developed.

Central and Northwestern Spain
In May 1981, hundreds of Spaniards were afflicted with a disease characterized by pneumonia and skin rashes. These symptoms were later associated with cooking oil contaminated with aniline—a poisonous organic chemical.

this dual emission, scientists have created machines that are much more complex than SPECT scanners. Called positron emission tomography, or PET, scanners, these machines rely on a dual set of detectors rotating around the patient. Because positron-emitting radioisotopes are extremely short-lived and cannot be kept in a storeroom awaiting use, PET scanners always work in conjunction with cyclotrons, a type of nuclear accelerator that can create the isotopes on the spot. In the future, longer-lived isotopes will be available.

So far, only a few major medical centers have installed these systems, which cost millions of dollars apiece. Nevertheless, PET has revolutionized the diagnosis of brain disorders, pinpointing abnormalities undetectable by other methods: tiny blockages in blood vessels (a precursor of strokes) hard-to-spot tumors, as well as the early chemical warnings of schizophrenia, manic depression, epilepsy and Alzheimer's disease. As more PET scanners come on line, they will provide insights into the metabolism of other organs as well.

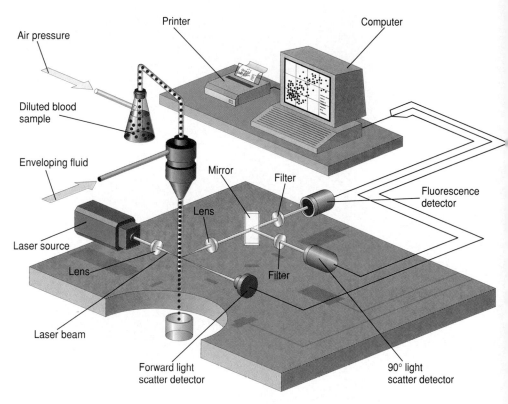

THE LAB TEST

Physicians of old who sniffed and tasted bodily fluids were performing a rudimentary chemical analysis. Nowadays, microscopes, chemical reagents and other sophisticated methods provide important clues—often undetectable by less precise means—to a patient's health. One of the best indicators is blood. Not only does it transport oxygen and other chemicals throughout the body, it also battles microbes and other harmful agents. Chemicals that are usually foreign to the bloodstream, or unusual amounts of normal substances, can indicate infection, poisoning, injury, malnutrition or disease.

With many blood tests, a little drop will do. Small samples are obtained by pricking a fingertip with the built-in needle of a "fingerstick" capillary tube; larger samples are usually drawn from a vein in the arm by needles attached to vacuum tubes. An anticoagulant may be added to the sample to prevent clotting. The most common blood test is the hematocrit, whose primary role is to determine the volume of packed red blood cells relative to the volume of whole blood. The sample is given a spin on a carousel called a centrifuge. As the horizontal test tube whirls around, centrifugal force pushes heavy particles toward the end of the tube. Three distinct layers appear: a mass of red cells on the bottom, a gray band of white cells and platelets in the middle and a large volume of yellowish plasma on top. An unusually low volume of red cells may signify anemia. Although red cell volume is the principal focus of the hematocrit, the test also shows the relative volumes

OPTICAL DETECTION DEVICE
Blood cells are grouped and counted by an automated optical detection device. The blood sample is focused into a stream by an enveloping fluid that concentrates the cells in single file. As the individual cells pass through a beam of laser light, each cell deflects the beam. Different cell types scatter the light in characteristic ways that are recorded by photodetectors. In addition to light scatter, fluorescent signals can also be measured when cells are tagged with appropriate dyes. A computer tallies the data and provides a census report in graphic form.

of other blood components: An increase in white cell volume can indicate leukemia; excessively yellow plasma can mean liver problems.

More specific information is obtained from a blood count, an inventory of the different types of cells in a given volume of blood. In one automated device, cells float one at a time through a small hole. Each cell causes a momentary rise in electrical resistance, which is registered by the machine.

A thousand times more numerous than all other blood cells, red cells contain hemoglobin, an iron-rich protein that is able to transport oxygen. A sharp drop in the red cell population indicates anemia, which can be an indicator of various problems, including hemorrhage, decreased red cell production in the bone marrow, dietary insufficiencies (iron, vitamin B_{12}, folate) or certain diseases such as lupus and rheumatic arthritis. Lung disease such as emphysema can raise counts.

Platelets, usually counted at the same time as red cells, also have an important role to play. Whenever there is a breach in a blood vessel, the platelets clump at the injury site to initiate clotting. A low platelet count can stem from leukemia, various autoimmune conditions, or exposure to chemicals such as DDT or some drugs; whatever the cause, a low population of platelets raises the risk of bleeding. An elevated count may be due to such causes as acute blood loss or various types of cancer; a high level increases the risk of heart attack and stroke. While a blood count is an efficient means of assessing health, diagnosticians must be wary of

The Home Test

Medical technology is now making inroads into the home, as exemplified by a new Japanese self-test device called the "Intelligent Toilet First Thing in the Morning." This familiar-looking installation is equipped with microelectronic sensors that measure urinary levels of sugar, protein, red and white blood cells and ketones—metabolites of fat that are indicative of liver function. Both blood pressure and body temperature can be measured simply by inserting a finger into a special hole on the side. Results of this early morning checkup are displayed five minutes later and may be sent by computer modem to a physician's office.

While the high-tech toilet is an extreme example, a growing array of simpler home test devices are available in drugstores. The timing of the fertile period in a woman's cycle can be anticipated with a urinalysis kit that demonstrates a color change if a certain hormone is present; another color reaction kit determines pregnancy. Diabetics can keep track of their blood glucose level by pricking a finger and dabbing blood on a test strip; the color change, indicative of blood glucose level, is interpreted by an electronic monitor.

Less expensive than laboratory tests, do-it-yourself testing can play an important role in patient health care. Still, regulatory boards have been reluctant to approve tests that may be administered incorrectly or whose results may be misinterpreted by nonprofessionals. Another concern is that results from some home tests, for sexually transmitted diseases for example, probably would not be reported to the health agencies that keep tabs on such cases. Though an AIDS home test is not yet available, the FDA is considering a model which would involved sending the kit back to a lab for testing. Results and counselling would be given anonymously over the phone.

However reliable the system, testing must not be confused with diagnosis, which is best left to the physician.

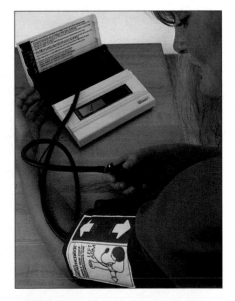

Many home testing products are designed for daily self-monitoring. This sphygmomanometer is used for checking blood pressure at home, precluding the anxiety associated with the doctor's office—a factor that can increase blood pressure. Regular monitoring also can aid in the fine-tuning of drug treatment for hypertension.

factors totally unrelated to disease which may alter the count. High altitude, for example, can boost the population of red blood cells; strenuous exercise can raise the platelet count.

The blood's white cells present the greatest counting challenge because they come in five main varieties. Sometimes physicians just order a simple count, which estimates total white cell population in a given volume of blood. An abnormally high number indicates the body is mobilizing against an infection. Most automatic analyzers recognize the five largest groupings of white cells—lymphocytes, eosinophils, basophils, monocytes and neutrophils—along with red cells and platelets. As the cells flow past a bright light, usually from a laser, each cell scatters the beam in a characteristic way.

Some analyzers have an optional feature that goes beyond counting the different white cell types and actually separates them physically. As the cells pass under a laser beam, the machine will assign a certain cell type an electrical charge. The charged cells are then deflected into a separate stream and collected for further testing. The appearance of abnormal white blood cells can indicate a number of conditions, including infectious mononucleosis.

SPECTROPHOTOMETRY

This technique is fundamental to clinical chemistry. Once a particular chemical has been detected in a solution, using a reagent that changes color on contact with the chemical, lab technicians then apply spectrophotometry to measure the chemical's concentration. White light is broken into its component colors by a monochro-

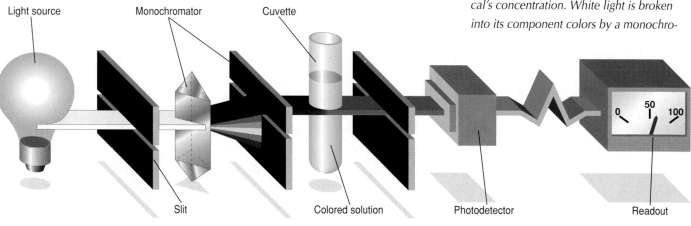

A test of the chemical content of blood is done on serum, the fluid left behind after whole blood has clotted and been centrifuged. Today's analytical machines check for a dozen or more chemicals at a time. At precisely the right time and temperature, the computer-controlled machine adds appropriate chemical reagents, incubates the samples, then shuttles them past a spectrophotometry scanner. The scanner measures the concentration of each chemical according to the sample's absorption of light of different wavelengths.

Blood proteins require special attention. Of the more than 100 proteins in human serum, five key groups are measured. The primary one is albumin, which transports hormones and helps maintain blood volume in vessels. The others are the four globulins—alpha 1 and 2, beta and gamma—integral parts of the immune system, especially of disease-fighting antibodies. In an ingenious technique called electrophoresis, blood serum is applied to a starchy or gel-like membrane, part of which is in contact with an electrically conducting solution; the solution is then connected to a power source for about an hour. Next, a stain reveals that the proteins have separated into distinct bands; the wider the band, the more molecules.

mator which then selects a specific wavelength of light. Chosen for its potential to be absorbed by the color of the reagent dye, this monochromatic light is then passed through the solution. The percentage of light absorbed is converted to an electrical signal by the photodetector. This information is conveyed to a visual readout, which indicates the concentration of the particular chemical in the solution.

The principal technique for measuring electrolytes is called potentiometry. First, a battery-like cell is created with a solution of electrolytes. Electrodes, inserted into the solution, read the potential—or voltage difference—of the solution, which contains different electrolytic substances such as potassium, chloride or sodium, as well as dissolved blood gases such as oxygen or carbon dioxide. Higher than normal concentrations produce a voltage increase; low concentrations, a drop from usual readings. Hormone levels, an indicator of glandular health, are measured by a nuclear medicine technique called the radioimmunoassay—or RIA. This test makes clever use of the body's natural ability to immobilize foreign invaders—antigens—by forming mirror-image compounds—antibodies—that link up with them in a lock-and-key fashion. The hormone in question, occurring naturally in the blood, is allowed to compete with a radioactively labeled quantity of the same substance in a contest to bind with the hormone's natural antibody. The resultant proportions of nonradioactive and radioactive hormone that attach to the antibody are used to calculate the hormone's level in the bloodstream.

Another optional test determines how well the patient's blood clots. The formation of clots is a complex process, involving five steps: constriction of the injured blood vessel to slow blood flow; gathering of platelets at the injury site; activation of a dozen chemicals known as coagulation factors; activation of chemicals that bring clotting to a close; and, finally, the gradual dissolution of the mesh-like clot. Inadequate clotting may be due to a number of conditions, from a buildup of anti-coagulant substances such as aspirin, to a range of maladies including heart or liver disease, leukemia, acute infection and hemophilia, the bleeder's disease that shadowed the descendants of Queen Victoria. In a manual test, a coagulant such as prothrombin or thromboplastin is mixed with a sample of venous blood; a stop-watch times the formation of a clot, which should appear in a few seconds. Other, semi-automated devices are sensitive to electrical or optical changes that signal the exact moment of coagulation.

Like blood, urine contains a host of chemical and biological substances that reflect health. In particular, metabolic wastes indicate how the kidney and liver are functioning. Color and turbidity offer quick visual evidence. A microscopic view may reveal casts—cylindrical bits of protein debris from the kidneys—as well as blood cells and skin cells, or crystals of chemicals. When ingredients in the urine elude vision—either direct or under magnification—laboratories turn to tiny dipsticks called reagent strips. Immersed in the urine sample, a chemical coating on the paper or plastic strip changes color on contact with the target material. Reagent strips are available for any number of possible urinary components. Proteins—normally present in immeasurable quantities—are sometimes a first hint of kidney disease; ketones, incompletely oxidized fatty acids, are a sign of diabetes or poor carbohydrate and fat metabolism; bilirubin, a breakdown product of certain cells, is normally removed by the liver—its presence indicates liver malfunction; nitrite, a bacterial waste, indicates infection. Some of the devices used to study blood help in the reading of reagent strips. The spectrophotometry scanner, for example, senses subtle changes of hue to which the human eye is colorblind. If chemical tests fail to get at the root of an illness, the physician may call on a specialist, called a pathologist, to make a direct examination of tissue. The pathologist is an expert in identifying cellular abnormalities, notably cancer.

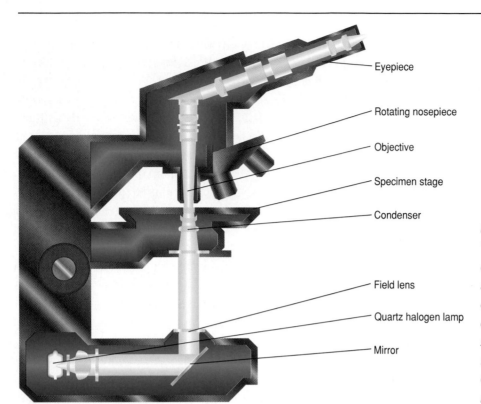

Eyepiece

Rotating nosepiece

Objective

Specimen stage

Condenser

Field lens

Quartz halogen lamp

Mirror

OPTICAL MICROSCOPE

The optical microscope renders minute objects visible through the use of light and lenses. High intensity light is directed by a mirror and field lens into a condenser, which focuses a beam on the specimen. The image is enlarged by lenses in the objective and the eyepiece. Clinical microbiologists and pathologists rely on this basic type of microscopy for the identification of microbes and cellular abnormalities. Various dyes are used to enhance detail, each highlighting particular cellular parts or types of tissue.

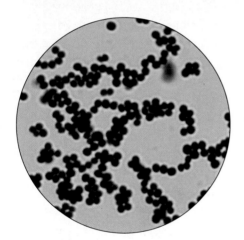

Staphylococcus aureus, a common cause of acute inflammation, is shown through bright field microscopy, a basic application of the optical microscope. A Gram stain, actually a series of stains, reveals particularities of bacterial structure.

Fluorescence microscopy, another optical technique, highlights *Salmonella typhi*. The causative bacteria of typhoid fever were stained with dyes that fluoresce in ultraviolet light.

First, though, the physician must take a sample, requiring different techniques depending on the tissue. Skin is often collected with nothing more than a little scraping; so are the cervical cells for a Pap smear, a common test for cervical cancer. However, for a deeper surface sample, physicians perform a "punch biopsy," cutting out a small, cylindrical plug with a coring device. Less accessible tissue must often be removed with a scalpel and surgical scissors while the patient is anaesthetized. If only a very small sample is required, a clump of cells can sometimes be retrieved at the end of a long, thin needle or through the hollow piping of a fiber-optic endoscope. Bone marrow samples are drawn, or aspirated, through

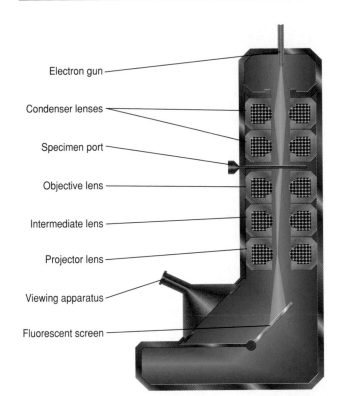

Electron gun

Condenser lenses

Specimen port

Objective lens

Intermediate lens

Projector lens

Viewing apparatus

Fluorescent screen

TRANSMISSION ELECTRON MICROSCOPE

Instead of light, the transmission electron microscope uses electrons—tiny particles carrying negative charges—to magnify images far beyond the power of optical microscopes. A series of magnets, called condenser lenses, focuses the electrons into a beam. On contact with the specimen, the electrons bounce off its surface, but are immediately focused by other lenses into an image on a fluorescent screen. Transmission electron microscopy is used when magnification of x10,000 or higher is required.

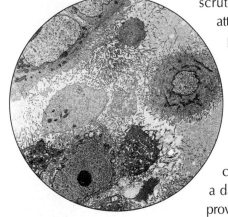

Electron microscopy, with its powerful magnifying capabilities, is used to detect mesothelioma, cancer in the abdominal cavity, in a tissue sample.

a thin, hollow needle usually inserted into the hipbone or breastbone. Specimens from the lungs, lymph nodes and thyroid also are sometimes aspirated.

To prepare a tissue specimen for microscopic examination, it first must be fixed and dried. Next, it is embedded in a hard, protective material—typically paraffin wax—and then sectioned into paper-thin slivers with a high-tech slicer called a microtome. Finally, the slivers are floated onto a glass slide, stained, dried again and covered with a thin glass shield. This painstaking process ordinarily takes several hours—much too long for a surgeon to wait for biopsy results while a patient lies on the operating table. The wait be shortened to a few minutes if the embedded tissue is quick-frozen, usually by placing it on a metal surface in a freezing unit, then rapidly made into a slide—a regular slide is also made soon after. The pathologist will examine the cells in the sample, checking to see if they are of normal size and shape, and whether particular cellular features occur in unusually great numbers.

Automated examining systems have been devised as a screening tool, exploiting the pattern-recognition capabilities of computers. A specimen slide is prepared, then it is scrutinized for abnormalities by a computer attached to a microscope. But, although computers can often distinguish between abnormal and normal cells, they have not proved 100 percent reliable. The final decision must still come from an experienced human observer.

For most tissue examinations, the pathologist uses a standard bright-field optical microscope—so called because it forms a dark image against a bright background. It provides magnification up to about 1,000 times. Some samples may contain cells whose distinguishing characteristics can only be rendered visible with the much greater magnifying power of electron microscopes—10,000 times or higher. A pathologist will often utilize an electron microscope in the identification of cancerous cells, for example. The potency of an electron microscope is also required to view objects significantly smaller than ordinary cells, such as viruses. Out of the domain of the pathologist, these minuscule invaders are identified by the keen eye of a different specialist, called a clinical microbiologist.

The physician may consult a clinical microbiologist if it is suspected that a patient's body may be host to tiny organisms known as microbes—bacteria, yeasts or viruses, for example. A common practice is to perform a "culture": taking a bodily specimen—perhaps a swab from the throat, a urine or blood sample or biopsy tissue—and creating an environment where putative microbes will be allowed to grow. Tests on bacteria or yeasts use a technique pioneered in the late 1800s by the German bacteriologist Robert Koch. A sampling of cells is spread over a gel-like nutrient called agar inside flat, circular glass containers known as petri dishes. The cells are then incubated at about body temperature, 98.6°F. After a day or so of dividing, each of the tiny, single-celled organisms will have grown into a separate colony. In many cases, the microbiologist relies on his naked eye, identifying specific microbes by their pattern of growth; a view of the microbes' structural particularities through an optical microscope will clarify any doubt.

Unlike cultured bacteria, the much smaller viruses may have to be examined directly, under an electron microscope. To culture a virus, which is unable to replicate outside a living cell, the agent has traditionally been injected into host animals or eggs containing a live embryo. Virologists have developed a simpler approach, using live cells in a petri dish as hosts. As the viruses take over cells, they form local areas of destruction, called plaques.

While the pathologist relies mainly on one variation of optical microscopy—bright field—the microbiologist may also use dark field and fluorescence microscopy. The dark field microscope, which uses a restricted light beam to render the specimen bright on a dark background, is useful in identifying certain microbes, such as *Treponema pallidum*, the causative agent of syphilis; the fluorescence microscope utilizes ultraviolet light to expose specimens which have been coated with fluorochrome dyes. Interestingly, some microbes are autofluorescing, lending themselves to fluorescence microscopy.

Before microbial specimens can be examined under a microscope, however, they must first be "fixed"—with heat or chemicals—and stained to bring out their internal structures. Often a bath in a common dye, such as methylene blue, will highlight a wide range of structures within a bacterial cell. But such simple staining will not distinguish among various kinds of bacteria in a culture. That requires a more complex technique, called differential staining. The most common example is the Gram stain, developed by the Danish physician Christian Gram in 1883. In the two-step process, cells are first stained with a crystal violet dye, then washed with an iodine solution. Those cells that retain the crystal violet after washing are called gram-positive; those that lose the dye are gram-negative. Finally, the smear is stained again, this time with safranin dye; gram-negative bacteria become pink or red, while gram-positive bacteria turn purple. Still other staining techniques highlight structures peculiar to certain bacteria, such as the internal protective coats visible in the genus *Clostridium*, responsible for a range of diseases, including botulism and tetanus.

Clinical labs are turning to automated systems to speed the identification of disease-causing bacteria. Working under computer control, these systems incubate specimens in separate compartments, clocking their rate of bacterial growth by measuring the output of carbon dioxide or changes in density. Some automatic systems can determine a microbe's susceptibility to different drugs. Such machines dis-

MOLECULAR ANTAGONISTS

The clinical test known as enzyme-linked immunosorbent assay (ELISA) is used to detect two important diagnostic clues that may be present in blood: Antigens are the chemical labels of microscopic invaders; antibodies are warriors of the immune system, able to lock on to specific antigens. Both of ELISA's two methods exploit the molecular lock-and-key relationship of the two antagonists, using one to expose the other.

DETECTION OF ANTIGEN	DETECTION OF ANTIBODY

Antibody for test disease is fixed to test plate.

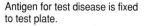

Antigen for test disease is fixed to test plate.

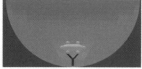

Blood serum sample is added; if antigen is present it will bind to antibody.

Sample is added; if antibody is present it will bind to antigen.

Enzyme-linked antibody is allowed to bind to antigen.

Enzyme-linked chemical antagonistic to antibody, called anti-gamma globulin, binds to antibody.

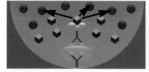

Chemical that reacts with enzyme is added; subsequent color change confirms presence of antigen.

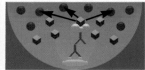

Chemical that reacts with enzyme is added; subsequent color change confirms presence of antibody.

tribute the infectious microbes among tiny wells, each of them containing a different antimicrobial drug. By monitoring the rates of growth in the wells, the machine can tell which drug will most effectively fight the microbe.

To test for microbes in the blood, diagnosticians often use a test known as ELISA—enzyme-linked immunosorbent assay. In one application, a specific immune antibody—designed to identify and attach itself to a specific microbe—is added to a blood sample; an added enzyme will cause the sample to change color if the disease-causing microbe is present. Conversely, the chemical label of the microbe, called the antigen, can be used to locate an antibody in the blood. The latter application is used to detect antibodies for the AIDS virus, HIV.

The newest, most sensitive test for microbes, and other causes of disease, involves so-called DNA probes. Located in the nuclei of all living cells, DNA—deoxyribonucleic acid—is the long, double-stranded helix that carries the basic hereditary message. If the structure of a microbe, say a bacterium, is known, scientists can create pieces of DNA identical to that of the microbe. The unknown bacterium can thus be identified in a similar way to matching nuts and bolts.

Still, even with the best of technology, diagnosis remains an art as well as a science. The doctor's judgment, alertness and creativity are at least as important as the tools at his command.

DNA PROBES

Interlocked like the two halves of a zipper, the complementary strands of deoxyribonucleic acid—or DNA—carry genetic information; a particular code can be the identifying marker of a specific genetic abnormality or a foreign invader, such as a virus. DNA probes can use such codes to diagnose a number of diseases. If a segment of DNA from a separated strand—in a sample of blood, say—locates a complementary segment in the form of a DNA probe, the two will link up. Scientists synthesize a piece of

DNA designed to match a segment of the DNA of the suspect, then label the probe with a radioactive substance. The suspect DNA is fragmented and spread onto a special membrane, to which it adheres. The DNA probe is added, then the membrane is rinsed; if the probe has not bound, it will wash away. The membrane is then placed on X-ray film. If the radioactively labeled segment has interlocked with DNA in the specimen, a black smudge appears, indicating that the suspect DNA is present.

MAGIC POTIONS

In October, 1977, a 23-year-old cook in a Somalian hospital came down with a fever. A rash erupted on his face, chest, arms—pimple-like dots that soon became engorged with pus. To everyone's astonishment, the man had smallpox. Two years earlier the World Health Organization had concluded a decade-long anti-smallpox campaign in which the dying man, Ali Maow Maalin, had worked as a volunteer vaccinator. By neglecting to vaccinate himself in his urgency to save others, he was destined to become a medical phenomenon: the last recorded case of smallpox anywhere on earth.

The first viable smallpox vaccine, in the 1790s, was itself a medical milestone. For centuries, people on various continents had practiced a rudimentary prophylaxis, scraping the pustules of a mildly infected patient, then dabbing the material in an eye of a healthy person. But all too often the treatment backfired, giving the "immunized" person a full-blown contagion. Then, an English country doctor named Edward Jenner noted an extraordinary fact: Milkmaids hardly ever contracted the dread virus. Usually, they had already caught a related disease called cowpox, whose only lasting effect on humans was to mobilize antibodies for various poxes, including smallpox. Jenner's inspiration lives on in the word vaccine, from the Latin *vacca*, for "cow."

Vaccines are just one of many types of drugs, a broad catch-all term including any substance used for the prevention, diagnosis or treatment of disease—sometimes just the relief of symptoms. While vaccines prepare the body's immune system to fight noxious invaders, many drugs are administered after an illness strikes. Drugs such as penicillin and other antibiotics, for example, fight infection by killing

Pellets tumble from an opened capsule, one of the most common devices used to administer a drug or a combination of drugs. The capsule's tasteless gelatin shell allows it to pass comfortably down the esophagus, postponing the dissolution until past the throat.

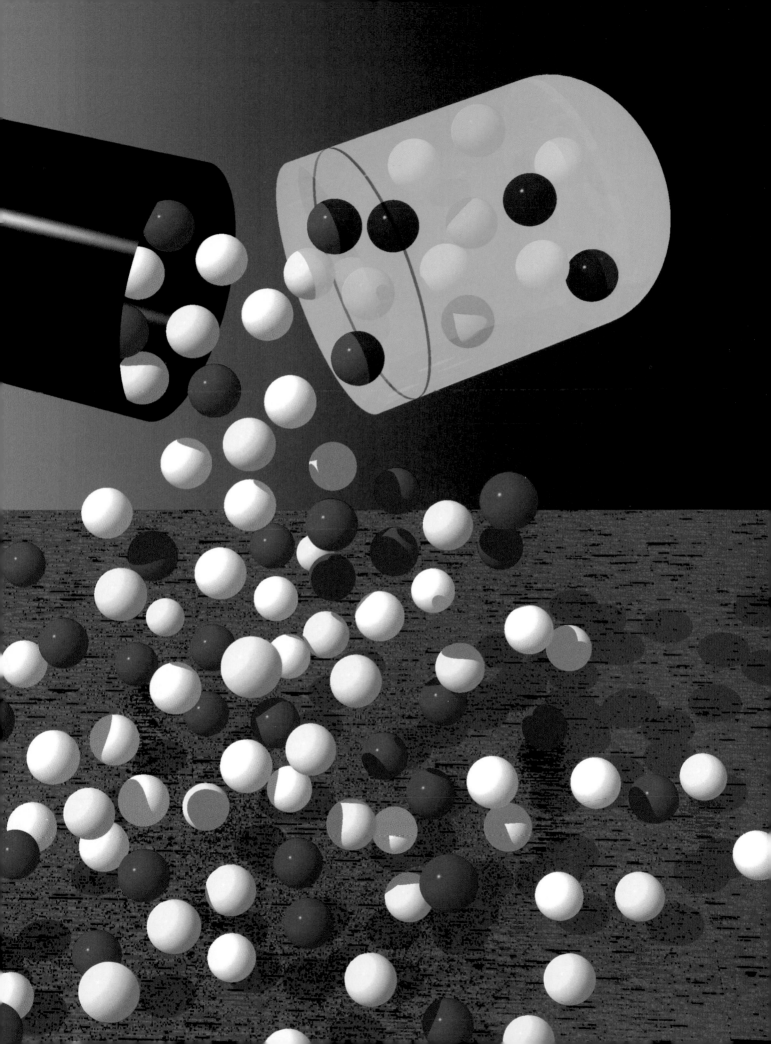

or immobilizing disease-causing organisms. Other drugs affect various systems of the body such as the nervous and endocrine systems, regulating hormones and similar biochemicals to promote health. One special category of drugs, designed for cancer victims, disrupts the growth of cancerous cells. And the body itself is equipped with an efficient natural defense mechanism—the immune system—that works 24 hours a day to fight off disease, and to preserve health among the body's more than 100 million million cells.

THE FRONT LINE OF DEFENSE

When the body is assaulted by a swarm of microbes—microscopic invaders including bacteria, viruses, protozoa and fungi—a special breed of white blood cells known as phagocytes spots the invaders and attacks, relentlessly gobbling the invaders. Unfortunately, the phagocyctes frequently cannot finish the job alone because while the microbes known as viruses are incapable of reproducing on their own, they quickly take over the reproductive systems of body cells; they then produce identical copies, or clones, of themselves, faster than the phagocytes can eat them. Specialized messenger phagocytes then leave the bloodstream to muster help in the lymphatic system, which produces another type of white blood cells

SELF-DEFENSE

The immune system protects the body from foreign invaders, such as bacteria and viruses, by means of an army of one trillion specialized white blood cells. Each type of cell has a specific task. For instance, some cells identify the enemy, others attack cells in which the enemy is hiding, while still others manufacture ammunition to be used in battle. The spleen is the main site of battle between invaders and the various white blood cells, as depicted during a virus onslaught (right).

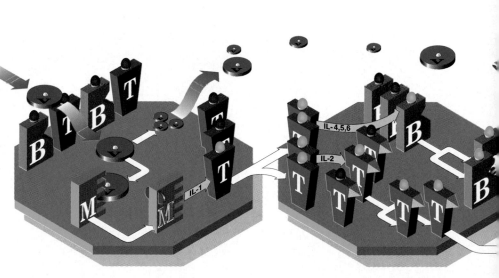

1. The Invasion
A virus invades the body, setting the battle in motion. At the front line of defense, a white blood cell called a macrophage devours the foreign invader and displays a viral fragment on its surface like a trophy. The marker, in conjunction with a chemical messenger called interleukin-1, or Il-1, later serves to activate a select group of white blood cells called helper Ts.

2. The Army Grows
The macrophage's message activates helper T cells into multiplying and releasing other chemical messengers—interleukins 2 through 5. These messengers call defenders to arms by stimulating the multiplication of killer T cells and other white blood cells called B cells; as well, they instruct some B cells to stop replicating and start producing antibodies—the guided missiles of the immune system which bind to and neutralize the enemy. Killer T cells will be responsible for destroying body cells that harbor the invading virus.

called lymphocytes. There are two groups of lymphocytes, T cells and B cells, and three types of T cells. One of the T types, aptly named killer Ts, releases deadly salvos of proteins that dispatch the infected cells by gnawing gaping holes in their membranes. Other T cells, helper Ts, do not attack directly; instead, they sound the alarm for B cells. B cells are lymphocyte warriors that systematically attack known enemies with their antibodies. Like guided missiles, antibodies seek out the microbes and lock on to them; some disarm the invaders, while others direct phagocytes to the microbes. The third group of T cells, supressor Ts, calls off the attack when the infection is contained. These maneuvers are possible only with the help of chemical messengers, including interleukin-1 and interleukin-2. Under such attack, most viruses hold out only a few days.

If the immune system seems to be losing ground in the battle, it can be made even more effective by drugs. Pharmacological intervention can boost, or in some cases tone down, the immune response. Recently, scientists have used the messenger chemicals of the immune system itself to develop a new arsenal of medicines. T and B cells respond to these drugs, known as immuno-enhancers, as they would to their own chemical commanders.

In September 1990, the medical press reported the results of a six-month study in which an immune system chemical called gamma interferon had been used to slash the number

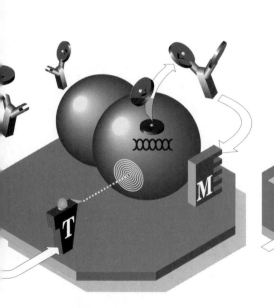

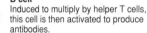
Red light
Indicates cell is not activated.

Green light
Indicates cell is activated.

Virus
A foreign invader that can cause disease, the virus is a parasite that must replicate in a living cell.

Helper T cell
Commander of the immune system, the helper T cell identifies the enemy and recruits other cells to help battle the infection.

B cell
Induced to multiply by helper T cells, this cell is then activated to produce antibodies.

Macrophage
The body's housekeeper, this phagocyte engulfs and digests foreign organisms, as well as calling helper T cells into the fray.

Antibody
A Y-shaped protein molecule, the antibody neutralizes the enemy by binding to viral proteins called antigens.

Killer T cell
A vicious killer, this cell specializes in destroying body cells that have been invaded by foreign organisms, and cells that have become cancerous.

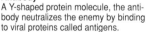
Suppressor T cell
Important after the battle has been won, this cell specializes in slowing down the activities of T and B cells once the infection is contained.

Memory cells
Generated during an attack, these cells continue to circulate in the body for years. Subsequent invasions of the same organism will cause memory cells to go into action.

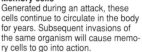

3. The Battleground
To accomplish its own goal, the virus must replicate inside a body cell, after which it must exit in order to infect other cells. The virus instructs the cell to manufacture viral genetic material—shown here as a twisted purple strand—and repackage it. Activated killer T cells attack virus-infected cells by puncturing the cell membrane chemically. The cell is destroyed, indirectly halting viral replication. Meanwhile, antibodies lock on to the virus, preventing it from infecting other cells. Macrophages play a second role in the battle at this point, by destroying the virus-antibody complex.

4. Victory
Once the viral threat is under control, suppressor T cells actively stop further cell activation and proliferation. Special killer T cells and B cells, called memory cells, stand ready to respond to any future invasion of the same virus. Finally, macrophages—which initiated the whole battle—die following the victory.

of infections due to an inherited immune deficiency called chronic granulomatous disease. Due to a lack of activation among the white blood cell immune troops, this devastating ailment results in persistent bacterial and fungal infections that lead to fibrous lumps on the skin, lungs and lymph nodes. Since gamma interferon activates the bacteria-devouring phagocytes, scientists correctly hypothesized that extra doses of the chemical might increase the appetite of the phagocytes, making them ravenous for bacteria. After six months of treatment, patients showed a 72 percent reduction in infections.

Another immune messenger, interleukin-2, is a potential cancer treatment. First, doctors remove the lymphocyte population from the patient's white blood cells. The lymphocytes are then incubated with interleukin-2, which enhances their killing power. Finally, the bolstered, more lethal lymphocytes are infused back into the bloodstream along with more interleukin 2. Although this experimental treatment has produced remission in only a limited number of cases, it is regarded as a step toward a promising new mode of pharmaceutical therapy for cancer.

Like interleukin-2, nearly all the new immuno-enhancers remain in the experimental stage. An exception is alpha interferon, which has received approval from the U.S. Food and Drug Administration—the governing body that scrutinizes all new drugs on the U.S. market. The drug, which enhances natural killer cell activity and modulates antibody responses, is prescribed for hairy cell leukemia, venereal warts and Kaposi's sarcoma—a skin cancer that frequently occurs in AIDS patients. It is expected to be approved for use in hepatitis B.

Occasionally, the immune system, instead of being strengthened with these immuno-enhancers, may need to be toned down with drugs called immunosuppressants. If, for instance, the immune system attacks an inappropriate target such as a transplanted organ, or the body itself, intervention is called for. Successful transplant surgery only became possible when the key to turning down the immune response was discovered. Previously, the new organ frequently succumbed to immune forces trained to destroy foreign matter. In 1978, a new drug called cyclosporine A made possible the first successful kidney graft, in Cambridge, England, by inhibiting the immune messenger chemical interleukin-2—the activator of T cells, and the major force behind organ rejection.

Cyclosporine is only one dramatic example of these new immunosuppressants. Frequently, these drugs are applied in the fight against auto-immune diseases—in which the immune system mistakes its own cells for foreign tissue. In crippling rheumatoid arthritis, for example, the immune system attacks cartilage and bone; in lupus erythematosus, the immune system attacks connective tissue and internal organs, resulting in scaling of facial skin, arthritis, progressive kidney damage and, often, deterioration of the heart, lungs and brain. The drug azathioprine is being used to treat both diseases. By depleting supplies of T and B blood cells, it manages to slow the immune system's misguided onslaught on the body. Inflammation, one of the main symptoms of auto-immune diseases, is treated by a family of drugs called anti-inflammatories. The most potent anti-inflammatories are naturally occurring hormones known as corticosteroids. Members of the same family as the bulk-producing anabolic steroids sometimes taken by athletes, these chemical messengers inhibit the action of T and B cells.

Further approval for immunosuppressants and immuno-enhancers depends, in part, on the development of measures to minimize the drugs' often harsh side

ANTIVIRAL DRUGS

The process of a virus' invasion of a healthy cell, the virus' reproduction and its exit from the cell comprises four stages, during any one of which antiviral drugs can attack. Some experimental antivirals thwart viral colonization altogether, either by blocking the virus' point of entry or by preventing the virus from shedding its protein coat, which houses DNA or RNA—the virus' genetic blueprint. Still others interfere with the synthesis of chemicals necessary for the virus to reproduce: the nucleic acids DNA or RNA—essential genetic material for each viral clone—or protein, a necessary viral building block. Finally, other antivirals may inhibit viral release from the cell, trapping newly created viral clones and thus preventing them from infecting other cells.

effects, which can sometimes outweigh their therapeutic benefits. Cyclosporine, for example, can damage the kidneys and liver; corticosteroids can cause problems as diverse as bone decalcification, leaky blood vessels, weight gain, fluid retention, diabetes and fragile skin. Yet, recognizing that such potent drugs will inevitably have a destructive effect on cells other than those targeted, chemists are getting round the problem for the moment by altering the way in which the drugs are administered. One method currently being used is to prescribe a drug mix, combining reduced doses of each immune-modifier so that no one drug is taken beyond its tolerable level.

IMMUNIZING AGAINST INVADERS

While adept at hunting down and killing enemies already at work in the body, immunology's real forte is in locking the door to invaders. Through vaccination, medical science has the potential to eradicate all infectious diseases, mainly caused by bacteria and viruses.

There are two types of immunization—active and passive—depending on how the vaccine goes to work in the body. In active immunity, the body is stimulated to produce its own antibodies to fight an invader, such as a bacterium or a virus. To achieve active immunity, the body first must be introduced directly to the invader—either through the infection itself or through a vaccine. One of the marvels of nature is that certain specialized blood cells—memory T and B cells—never forget an invader. Thereafter, recognizable foes are greeted with a deadly counter-attack. Jenner's milkmaids, for example, had developed immunity to cowpox because their memory T and B cells recognized the cowpox virus; because the smallpox virus is similar in shape, it too was treated as a harmful alien. In the case of vaccines, a totally disarmed bacterium or virus is used to create the vaccine. Antigens in the vaccine, when injected into the body, stimulate the formation of antibodies that react to eradicate that antigen. Vaccines can be made either by rendering the infectious organism totally powerless, or by robbing it of enough strength that—though not completely incapacitated—it is incapable of causing the disease.

While active immunization against bacteria, such as those that cause whooping cough and typhoid, is generally successful, there are exceptions. Viruses are not fended off so easily by vaccines because they can elude memory cells by changing their shapes. The rhinoviruses that cause the common cold, for instance, mutate by rearranging the proteins on their outer envelope, rendering any putative cold vaccine obsolete almost immediately. HIV, the AIDS virus, mutates in a similar way: By shifting its protein envelope, it creates entire new strains; so far more than 20 have been isolated.

Risks, though rare, can be deadly. In Berkeley, California, in the mid-1950s, a supposedly completely disarmed virus was used by Dr. Jonas Salk in the first effective vaccine against polio. But because one batch of the virus had not been properly deactivated—and thus was still active—the vaccine infected 260 people,

VIRAL LIFE CYCLE

Cell
Virus must colonize cell in order to reproduce.

DNA or RNA

Protein molecule

Viral clone before addition of protein coat

1. Penetration
Virus enters cell.

2. Removal of protein coat
Naked virus can now use its genetic material to reproduce.

3. Production of protein and genetic material
Virus uses cell's chemical machinery to manufacture protein (a necessary component of new viruses) and either DNA or RNA (genetic material essential to viral reproduction).

4. Release of viral clones
Newly assembled viruses exit, ready to colonize other cells.

of whom 10 died. In the aftermath of this tragedy, Dr. Albert Sabin developed a weakened vaccine, the completely safe and efficient polio vaccine in use today.

Unlike these two forms of active immunity, which mobilize the body's immune system to produce its own antibodies, passive immunity introduces antibodies directly into the bloodstream to fight the invader. These antibodies can be extracted from an antiserum prepared in vast quantities in large animals such as horses. Although passive immunity usually fades away after only a few weeks—unlike active immunity, which may last a lifetime—it is nevertheless a useful treatment following contact with a life-threatening infectious agent or toxin. This strategy, called immunotherapy, is used against rabies, tetanus and sometimes even cancer.

ATTACKING INVADERS DIRECTLY

While the body's immune system is a powerful defense against infectious disease—especially when assisted by immune system modifiers or vaccines—more aggressive means are required at times. Antimicrobials, a family of drugs with two branches—antibacterials and antivirals—bypass the immune system entirely, attacking and destroying invaders directly. Many bacterial infections, such as syphilis, used to carry a high death risk, almost like the AIDS virus today. During

The War Against Bacteria

Bacteria, among the smallest life forms on Earth, thrive successfully in the most inhospitable places and adapt quickly to new conditions in order to survive. For the human body, once they gain entry, bacteria mean infection. Antibacterial drugs do put a halt to their reproduction and even destroy bacteria, but although drugs such as penicillin and tetracycline have proved effective against bacterial infections for some time now, some new strains of bacteria have appeared that resist these drugs.

Drug resistance, as explained by microbiologists, is a dictum of evolution: The longer a bacterium is exposed to a certain drug, the more likely it is to develop resistance. Bacteria pull out all the stops in order to resist drugs. They may release special enzymes that render a drug impotent or change their outer membranes so that a drug cannot gain entrance. They can even alter their internal structure so that they are no longer susceptible to the

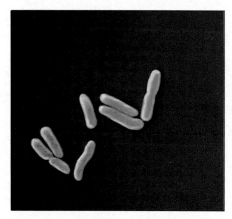

Pseudomonas aeruginosa bacteria are shown above, more than 20,000 times life size, reproducing in a culture dish. Although they are minute (250,000 bacteria would fit into an

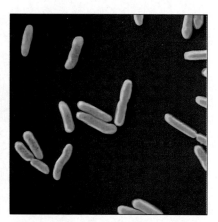

area the same size as the period at the end of this sentence), bacteria are extremely productive, dividing every 10 minutes in conditions favorable to them.

drug. Not surprisingly, penicillin, discovered in 1928 and the first drug to be used against bacteria, was also the first antibacterial drug to become a casualty in this war.

Many researchers blame the availability of inexpensive antibacterial drugs, claiming that they are administered so often that the bacteria learn to evade them. For example, meat products are an insidious source of the antibiotic tetracycline. The use of animal feed that has been treated with the drug, which fosters growth in livestock, also has

the effect of promoting resistance to this drug in humans. With the diminution of drug effectiveness, it is becoming increasingly difficult to find new medical ammunition to fight infection. Often, individuals being treated for bacterial infections such as gonorrhea are given a combination of antibacterial drugs with the hope that if one doesn't work, another might. In the meantime drug designers are scrambling to produce a new generation of effective antibacterial drugs.

THE BACTERIAL CELL

Cell membrane
Selective gateway
to the cell's interior

Protein molecule
Cellular building block

Cell wall
Protective coat

DNA—Deoxyribo-nucleic acid
Vital genetic
information

ANTIBACTERIAL DRUGS

A bacterial cell, such as the one shown in cross section above, can be targeted by antibacterial drugs either by inhibiting the formation of the protective cell wall; by disrupting the selective permeability of the cell membrane—an essential gateway for substances entering or leaving the cell; or by tampering with the synthesis of vital bacterial components such as protein and the nucleic acid DNA—essential for cellular reproduction. Many antibacterials are directed at structures that exist only in bacterial cells, and therefore do not harm the cells of the body. Penicillin, for instance, binds to an enzyme necessary for the formation of the bacterial cell wall—a feature which is absent in mammalian cells. Other drugs act on bacterial ribosomes—necessary for protein synthesis—which are different from mammalian ribosomes. Yet another group of antibacterials attack lipids—fatty material—within the cell membrane.

the last half century, antibacterials have crippled countless such diseases, waging war principally on bacteria, but also on other microbes such as fungi.

Antibacterials attack bacteria at one of four vulnerable targets: the cell wall, the cell's protective membrane, its proteins or either of its two nucleic acids—deoxyribonucleic acid (DNA) and ribonucleic acid (RNA)—both of which are essential to cell reproduction and the synthesis of protein. It is the latter mechanism—attacking nucleic acids—that made the antibacterials known as sulfonamides the first drugs to triumph over microbial invaders in the 1930s. Although bacteria are not killed by sulfonamides, they are rendered incapable of reproducing. Despite a gradual loss of effectiveness as common bacteria have developed a resistance to sulfonamides, the drugs are still in use, especially in the treatment of urinary tract infections and certain infections occurring in AIDS patients.

The most famous antibacterial is penicillin. Unlike sulfonamides, which effectively sterilize microbes, penicillin kills them outright. Because bacteria contain a large volume of water, they require a rigid outer cell wall to keep them from bursting; penicillin prevents special proteins called enzymes from building these cell walls. Construction comes to a halt and the cell dies an early death.

Other important bacterials include drugs such as tetracyclines and polymyxins. Tetracyclines are effective in the treatment of bronchitis and pneumonia and are a useful alternative for patients who are allergic to penicillin. Polymyxins are useful in the treatment of skin infections.

The other branch of the antimicrobial family, antivirals, deals with the mysterious and stubborn invaders called viruses. These microbes are inherently more difficult to kill than other bacteria, mainly because while they are capable of killing, viruses are not, technically speaking, alive. One step down the evolutionary chain from the very simplest of bacteria, viruses are not even cells, but merely blueprints for their own reproduction. Yet while they are unable to reproduce or even maintain themselves independently, they manage to exist by hijacking the genetic machinery of cells and using it to replicate themselves by the thousands—often killing the host cell in the process. The challenge is to neutralize the parasite without harming the cell.

Antivirals, which arrived on the pharmaceutical market only two decades ago, utilize three strategies: They either thwart the virus from entering the cell, inhibit it from replicating or prevent viral clones from leaving the host cell.

The first tactic is employed against the flu virus. Like many viruses, the flu virus has an outer fatty lipid sheath. Its first objective is to slough off this sheath, then permeate a cell with its genetic blueprint, in this case strands of RNA—ribonucleic acid. Drugs such as amantadine and rimantadine act as straitjackets, preventing the virus from shedding its lipid coat.

The drug AZT—azido dioxythymidine—fights AIDS by using the second tactic of antivirals. It prevents reproduction of the HIV virus believed to cause AIDS. HIV belongs to a category of viruses that must undergo a chemical transformation before ensconcing themselves in a cell. These viruses, some of which cause cancer, use RNA as their genetic template. The RNA, however, must be converted into DNA before reproduction can take place. This conversion is dependent on a special enzyme called reverse transcriptase. AZT wears a molecular mask that distracts reverse transcriptase from its proper target; because RNA is never converted to DNA, the virus cannot reproduce.

Viruses that use DNA directly as their genetic blueprint can similarly be prevented from reproducing thanks to the drug acyclovir. The most effective antiviral drug yet developed, acyclovir is used for herpes-related ailments, including cold sores, genital herpes, shingles and chickenpox.

The final stage at which viruses are vulnerable is when they have reproduced and are ready to colonize other healthy cells. Before new viruses can bind to other cells, they first must be prepared by enzymes that attach carbohydrate molecules to their protein surfaces. New drugs, known as enzyme-inhibitors, block this process and are being used in experimental AIDS treatment.

ALTERED SIGNALS

While many drugs work by attacking invaders directly, others engage in a kind of chemical subterfuge: They rewrite the signals of the body's nervous and endocrine systems. Drugs that act on the central nervous system, such as cocaine or caffeine, alcohol or antidepressants, all modify communication between nerve cells, or neurons, largely within the brain. At the point where one neuron makes contact with another lies a microfine space called the synaptic gap, across which one neuron sends a chemical message, called a neurotransmitter. Some drugs intervene before the chemical message makes it across the synapse—affecting the synthesis, storage, metabolism or release of neurotransmitters; others step in afterward—mimicking the neurotransmitter's message or blocking the site where the message is normally delivered. The tranquilizer diazepam (Valium), for example, increases the effect of GABA, a neurotransmitter that tones down communication

NERVOUS SYSTEM DRUGS

Drugs can alter nervous signal transmission in a variety of ways, including mimicry of a normal chemical message. If the drug's molecular structure is sufficiently similar to that of a particular neurotransmitter—a chemical messenger that passes information from one nerve cell to the next—it can trigger a response in cells with which the neurotransmitter usually communicates. The painkilling drug morphine, as shown in the diagram below, has a similar structure to that of endorphins—the brain's natural opiates that suppress pain in moments of great stress.

NATURAL OPIATE

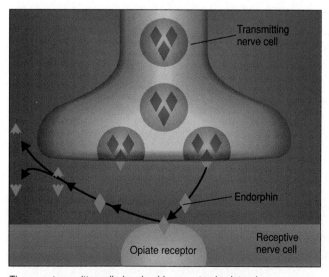

The neurotransmitter called endorphin—a natural opiate—is released from a transmitting nerve cell. It travels to a neighboring nerve cell and binds to an opiate receptor on the cell's surface. After the endorphin has delivered its message—"Block pain signals"—it is subsequently destroyed.

OPIATE DRUG

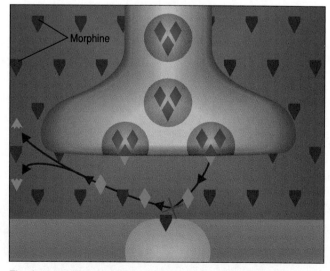

The drug morphine—an opiate derived from the poppy plant—floods the area between the transmitting and receptive nerve cells. Morphine binds to the opiate receptor, delivering a similar painkilling message to that of the endorphin.

with other neurons. Consequently, the brain is lulled and the patient feels calm. Morphine, a standard painkilling drug, does its work by binding to the brain's opiate receptors. Normally these receptors are activated by the brain's natural painkillers, called endorphins.

Antidepressant drugs modify communication within the central nervous system to improve the mood of depressed individuals. Many antidepressants boost one or both of the neurotransmitters serotonin and noradrenaline, each of which is involved in the regulation of mood. But these drugs inadvertently can cause undesired repercussions such as blurred vision, dry mouth and constipation.

Another class of drugs acts on the autonomic nervous system, rewriting the messages that control unconscious body functions. The system's two divisions, sympathetic and parasympathetic, carry out complementary duties. The sympathetic nervous system primes the body for action by constricting the arteries, accelerating the heart, dilating the pupils. Conversely, the parasympathetic division ensures that the heart is slowed down, blood pressure is lowered and nutrients are digested.

One well-known family of drugs that opposes the effects of the sympathetic nervous system is called beta-blockers. So-named because they block specific neurotransmitter receptors called beta-receptors, these drugs reduce the excitatory effect of the neurotransmitter noradrenaline on the heart. Millions rely on beta-blockers to counter high blood pressure, cardiac pain or arrhythmias.

The drug pilocarpine, used to treat glaucoma, mimics the action of the parasympathetic nervous system by stimulating the opening of the eyes' drainage canals for ocular fluid. The action reduces pressure within the eyeball, thus saving sight.

The body's second major communications network is the endocrine system. Whereas the nervous system communicates principally through neurotransmitters, the endocrine system relies exclusively on hormones that circulate in the blood. The pituitary gland, under control of the brain region known as the hypothalamus, releases hormones that travel either to other endocrine glands—ordering them to synthesize or release their own hormones—or directly to nonglandular tissues that depend on endocrine messages for metabolic instructions. Endocrine drugs are often used to compensate for an excess or a deficiency of a certain hormone.

As with many body systems, endocrine activity is most apparent when it goes awry. If the pancreas cannot produce the hormone insulin, for instance, a deranged metabolism results; insulin injections restore order, saving the diabetic patient from elevated blood glucose levels which can lead to coma and even death. A deficiency of the hormone calcitonin, whose job is to limit the amount of calcium

ENDOCRINE SYSTEM DRUGS

Drugs that interact with the body's endocrine system function by mimicking or inhibiting natural hormones. Synthetic insulin, for example, is used to treat diabetic patients who lack sufficient natural insulin. Here, synthetic insulin is shown binding with its receptor on the surface of an insulin-sensitive cell—in this case, a skeletal muscle cell (purple). The insulin causes the cell to be more easily permeated by glucose that is circulating in the blood (red), and activates enzymes that help the cell store energy in a more complex form than glucose.

Stored energy
Released as glucose when needed by the body

Activated enzyme
Promotes glucose storage

Skeletal muscle cell
Absorbs and stores glucose

Hormone receptor
Binds insulin

Synthetic insulin
Replaces natural insulin for diabetic patients

Blood capillary
Transports glucose throughout the body

Glucose molecule
Enters cells more easily in the presence of insulin

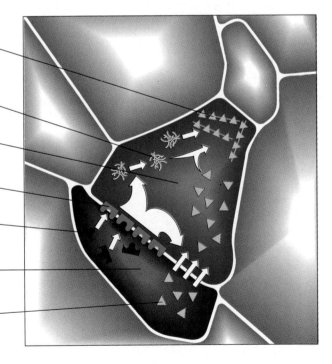

released into the blood from bone, leads to osteoporosis—decreased bone mass. Synthetic calcitonin can be administed to treat osteoporosis.

Some endocrine drugs take on tasks beyond the repair of hormonal malfunctions. The birth control pill prevents conception by influencing levels of the hormone estrogen. While a woman is pregnant, the endocrine system naturally subverts the release of further eggs from the ovary, thus ensuring that no new eggs can be fertilized during the pregnancy. The pill produces the same effect, essentially fooling the body into thinking that it is already pregnant.

FIGHTING CANCER

Whether tampering with chemical messages or combating invaders, each of the various families of drugs has a specialty appropriate to the ailments it treats. Quashing rampant cell growth is the specialty of antineoplastics, the drugs used in fighting the more than 250 different kinds of cancer. Antineoplastics disrupt a cell's life cycle during one or more of its four stages: resting; initiation of production of the RNA essential to the manufacture of protein; increase in production of the DNA that regulates all aspects of the cell's life; and mitosis, or cell division.

Alkylating agents such as nitrogen mustard are the pharmaceutical descendants of military mustard gas; these agents sabotage the synthesis of DNA. Autopsies of World War I mustard gas victims showed destruction of the bone marrow—ordinarily among the fastest-growing normal cells in the body. Further investigation revealed that a highly reactive part of the drug molecule had interacted with the chemical components of DNA, totally disrupting the third stage of the cell's cycle and leaving it with no genetic blueprint. Stage four, cell division, could not follow. Researchers wondered if this lethal force could be unleashed on cancer cells without killing the patient. The answer was yes. Nitrogen mustard proved useful in the treatment of various types of cancer, including certain leukemias. Today, it has been largely supplanted by the more stable cyclophosphamide, currently the most commonly prescribed alkylating agent; cyclophosphamide is often used in the treatment of leukemias and cancer of the lymph glands.

Other cancer-killing drugs, called antimetabolites, are less precise in their aim; they attack during both stages two and three of the cell cycle. Their method is to sneak into the cell under the guise of the chemicals that normally perform essential metabolic processes, preventing these processes. One of these antimetabolites, cytosine arabinoside, is derived from sea sponges. It combats an acute form of leukemia by inhibiting the action of an enzyme necessary to produce or repair DNA. Yet another, 5-fluorouracil—used to treat breast and gastrointestinal cancer—masquerades as a certain type of nucleic acid building block; abnormal proteins result and DNA synthesis in the cancerous cells comes to a halt.

Some breast and lung cancers have responded well to certain drugs that interfere with stage four of the cell cycle—division, or mitosis. Aptly named mitotic inhibitors, the drugs are derived from the periwinkle plant.

The drugs known collectively as antitumor antibiotics are developed from natural chemicals found in fungi. Scientists discovered that fungi, like many living organisms, have a natural system for defending themselves from predators. Antitumor antibiotics use fungal defense chemicals to treat cancers in the head, neck, testicles, lung, breast and ovaries.

Also playing a major role in cancer treatment are hormones, which exploit the hormone dependency of some cancers. The prolific growth of tumor cells found in a number of breast cancers, for example, is linked to the hormone estrogen. The antihormone tamoxifen binds to receptors for estrogen on certain cancerous cells, starving the tumor of this important growth agent. Other antihormones interfere with the production of testosterone, a hormone responsible for male characteristics, and are used for palliative therapy in advanced prostate cancer.

The quest for more refined cancer cures has also led scientists into immunotherapy. Experimental cancer vaccines differ from regular vaccines—such as the one for smallpox—in that those inoculated already have the disease. Researchers hypothesize that disarming tumor

CANCER CHEMOTHERAPY

DNA is the target of the drug group called antineoplastics, used to treat cancerous cells. The vital genetic information contained in DNA is located in the cell's nucleus in the form of twisted rope ladders (right). If DNA is severely damaged or destroyed, the cell can no longer reproduce. Antimetabolites, alkylating agents, antitumor antibiotics and mitotic inhibitors, the four main antineoplastics, work by interfering with DNA (below).

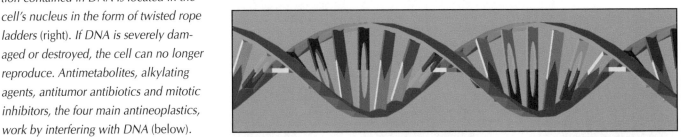

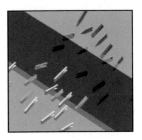

1. Antimetabolites
Inhibit the synthesis of DNA by a number of disruptive actions, including substituting for DNA components; thus these components do not fit together properly.

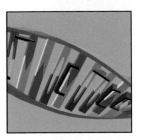

2. Alkylating agents
Create permanent cross-links both within and between DNA strands, inhibiting strand separation necessary for cell division.

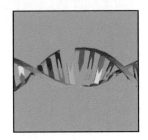

3. Antitumor antibiotics
Disrupt DNA by a variety of different mechanisms, including breaking DNA strands.

4. Mitotic inhibitors
Block mitosis, or cell division, by inhibiting the separation of chromosomes—threadlike structures composed of DNA.

cells and reinjecting them into the patient may bolster the immune system, prodding its natural killer T cells to destroy existing tumors. Clinical trials involving the skin cancer known as malignant melanoma are under way.

Another experimental treatment seeks to kill tumors by cutting off their plumbing lines. In order to satisfy their ravenous appetites and wash away their wastes, tumors extend a dense network of blood vessels in a process called angiogenesis. This process contributes to the tumors' formidable strength and capacity for growth. Recently, however, scientists have discovered a number of proteins that turn off the angiogenesis factor—a chemical that permits tumors to make blood vessels faster than can normal tissue. In animal models researchers have starved tumors to death by cutting off their blood supply.

Finally there are cases where drugs conceived for other purposes prove useful in the war against cancer. The drug verapamil was first used in the treatment of, among other things, abnormal heart rhythms. By blocking a sort of bailing pump believed to expel anticancer drugs from certain cancer cells, verapamil has produced some remissions in patients with myeloma—cancer of the bone marrow.

For all their cancer-killing efficiency, the disadvantage of antineoplastics is that they strike not only cancer cells, but also healthy cells. Particularly vulnerable are those cells that normally grow and divide rapidly, as in the bone marrow, hair follicles and gastrointestinal tract. Taking such drugs thus results in anemia, hair loss and nausea. Cancer drug therapy, then, must follow a strategy of quick attacks followed by a waiting period. "Drug cocktails" combine different drugs, in an attempt to avoid administering any one drug beyond its maximum tolerated dose.

HOMING IN ON THE TARGET

The problem of liquidating enemies without injuring bystanding cells and tissues is one of the most important goals of all drug delivery systems. This concern has spawned innovative targeting mechanisms such as monoclonal antibodies—bio-

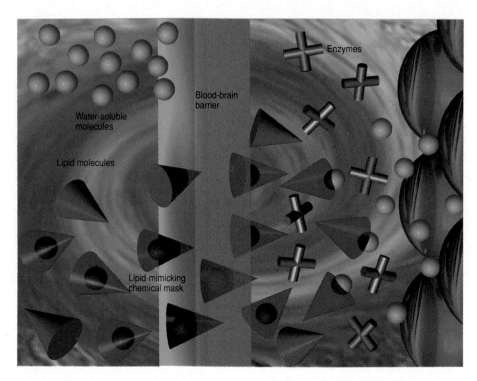

logical guided missiles. All antibodies have the ability to seek out and cling to a known antagonist—the chemical labels known as antigens—making them useful in drug targeting. Antibodies are mass produced by injecting mice with the antigen for which antibodies are required, then harvesting antibody-producing cells from the mouse spleens. These cells are then fused with cancer cells growing in a tissue culture. Doing what cancer cells do best, they proliferate and secrete limitless antibody clones—the cloned antibodies, however, possess none of the cancer cells' malignant properties. Next, an added toxic payload increases the antibodies' killing power, placing them in the category known as "magic bullets."

Monoclonal antibodies are also being used to prevent rejection after bone marrow grafting by blocking the immune system's T cells from attacking the grafted material—in some cases, the grafted marrow attacks its host, a problem treated by immunosuppressive drugs. Monoclonals are being tested in cancer treatment and may soon be used for rheumatoid arthritis and inflammatory bowel disease.

LIPOSOME DRUG TRANSPORT

Used to transport drugs, a liposome is a microscopic sphere composed of concentric layers of lipid molecules—fatty material. As seen in the cross section (above), one end of each lipid molecule is attracted to fat and its other end is attracted to water; lipids in an aqueous environment spontaneously assume an end-to-end configuration. Fat-soluble drugs (shown as green squares) can be entrapped within the lipid layers; water-soluble drugs (yellow squares) can be entrapped in the watery medium between the lipid layers. The drug molecules are released in the body when phagocytes—a type of white blood cell—consume the liposome, destroying its structure and spilling its contents.

Lipid molecule

Watery medium

Water-soluble drug

Fat-soluble drug

Monoclonal antibodies and other magic bullets seek out and destroy with reasonable success. Still, they remain ineffective in treating diseases of the brain, which is protected by the biochemical roadblock known as the blood-brain barrier. The brain depends on blood vessels to deliver oxygen and glucose for fuel, amino acids for neuronal growth, and iron for cell metabolism—if all the brain's capillaries were laid end-to-end, they would stretch 500 miles, the width of Kansas. This circulatory highway transports a wide variety of chemicals—necessary to the rest of the body—that could be harmful to the brain. Blood vessels in the brain, therefore, have exceptionally tight and selective walls. Made of the fatty materials known as lipids, these walls permit the passage only of substances that can dissolve in fat. Lipid-soluble drugs such as antidepressants and certain tranquilizers cross the barrier with ease. So do alcohol and nicotine. By and large, though, most effective drugs are water soluble, not lipid soluble, and so cannot penetrate the barrier. But treating brain disease is a monumental concern.

One experimental approach is to flood the barrier with a substance that renders it permeable. The drug mannitol is injected into the carotid arteries, on the side of the neck, which pump blood directly into the capillary system of the brain. Mannitol softens up the blood vessel walls by drawing water out of cells, shrinking them and loosening the connections between them. Intravenous drugs follow, slipping through the weakened barrier.

Another, more established solution is to disguise a raw material with a chemical mask that is soluble in fatty materials; once inside the brain, the raw material is absorbed and converted into the desired compound. Such a drug is called a prodrug—literally meaning "before drug," since the substance technically becomes a drug only at the moment the brain acts upon it. An example is levodopa, used by sufferers of Parkinson's disease. After successfully crossing the blood-brain barrier by wearing a lipid mask, levodopa is transformed into dopamine, the neurotransmitter responsible for the fine muscle movements lost to Parkinson's patients.

SPECIAL DELIVERY

Pharmacologists, as well as determining how to permeate barriers and reach their target, are increasingly concerned with keeping drug doses constant. Traditional methods, such as tablets and injections, often deliver a single megadose. Controlled delivery smoothes out the extremes of drug dosage.

One of the simplest and gentlest drug packaging methods uses liposomes, structures composed of concentric layers of fatty material—also found in body cells—interspersed with watery layers. According to one theory, liposomes are devoured by the white blood cells called phagocytes in the lymph nodes, spleen and liver; the liposome's structure is believed to collapse, releasing the drug into the bloodstream. One aerosol spray, now used experimentally to combat a form of pneumonia occurring in AIDS patients, uses liposomes that carry pentamidine—a drug that attacks the causative parasite.

Working cooperatively with the new generation of chemical drug carriers are a host of innovative devices that simplify drug delivery and administration. One such device is the transdermal patch, an unassuming flesh-colored strip that could easily be confused with a bandage. In reality, it contains a drug that is able to pass through its membrane. The patient need only apply the patch, and the drug begins to seep through the skin at a rate regulated by the membrane, similar to an intravenous drip without the needle.

The patch offers four great advantages over other drug delivery systems. Because the drug passes directly through the skin to the bloodstream, absorption is quick, meaning lower doses and, hence, fewer side effects. The drug's constant flow evens out the peaks and troughs of chemical concentration associated with tablet medications. The patch is easily applied to nauseated or unconscious patients who might be incapable of swallowing medication. Finally, if the patch produces undesirable side effects, it can be removed very simply.

With such patches, angina pectoris patients, who used to take nitroglycerine tablets to combat cardiac pain now can get an even dose all day long. Doctors are finding that this way of delivering nitroglycerine actually helps prevent angina attacks: Because the drug keeps the coronary arteries dilated over a long period of time, there are fewer occasions when the heart muscle is getting less oxygen than it needs. Other potential cargo for the patch includes pain-relieving drugs of all kinds, hormones—either as contraceptives or as supplements for postmenopausal symptoms—and a transitional supply of nicotine to help smokers kick the habit. A distinct disadvantage of the transdermal patch is that it works only with drugs that are sufficiently fat-soluble to diffuse through the skin. Similar to the blood-brain barrier, skin is impermeable to highly water-soluble drugs.

The state of the art in the delivery of oral medications is the osmotic pill, which dissolves drugs stored in solid form by using the natural principle of osmosis. Water passes through a semipermeable membrane from a solution of lower concentration to one of higher concentration. Thus, dilute fluids from the gastrointestinal tract pass through the pill's semipermeable membrane and dilute its highly concentrated contents, which then flow out into the gastrointestinal tract through a tiny hole. Medications for asthma and hypertension are beginning to appear in osmotic pill form. An important advantage of the osmotic pill over traditional tablets or capsules is that the rate of drug release is not significantly affected by changes in stomach

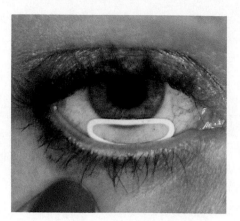

Placed directly beneath the lower eyelid, an ocular insert delivers the drug pilocarpine, used to treat glaucoma. The insert releases a steady drug dose over the span of a week, reducing pressure within the eyeball and preserving eyesight.

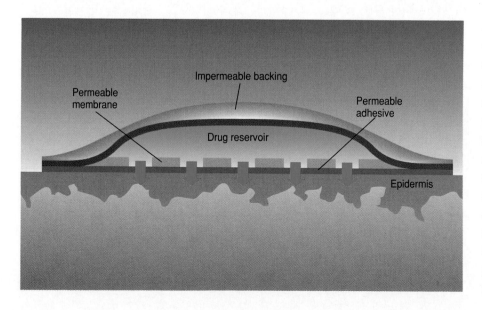

Permeable membrane

Impermeable backing

Permeable adhesive

Drug reservoir

Epidermis

TRANSDERMAL PATCH

One of the most successful drug delivery systems, the patch allows drugs to seep through the epidermis—the outermost layer of the skin. The thin, flexible patch typically contains four layers: an impermeable backing, a drug reservoir, a permeable membrane that controls the rate of delivery and an adhesive—also permeable. While severe side effects can result from digestion or injection of substances such as the anti-motion sickness drug scopolamine—often taken up to six times daily—a patch can provide a moderate dose, with reduced side effects, for up to three days.

acidity or by the presence of food. Once again, the patient avoids the peaks and valleys of conventional oral medications. One disadvantage is that the osmotic pill's membrane is insoluble and must be excreted through the bowel. In some older patients with diverticular disease—pouches or sacs in the intestine—this can present a problem.

Another approach to controlled release uses capsules containing drug pellets with varying rates of absorption. Some pellets dissolve in the stomach's acids, whereas others are acid-resistant and dissolve only with the aid of intestinal enzymes. These capsules are used in a multitude of applications, including cold medications.

Making a little drug go a long way, implantable slow-delivery systems are longer-term solutions to drug delivery. One is a new contraceptive IUD—intrauterine device. About an inch-and-a-half long, this T-shaped device is a reservoir which, when implanted in the uterus, diffuses a steady dose of the hormone progesterone. This hormone exerts a contraceptive effect by disrupting the uterine lining and thus preventing the attachment of fertilized eggs. With such direct delivery systems, very low dosages are required.

Other delivery systems use pumps—either worn externally and connected to the bloodstream by a catheter or implanted inside the body. External pumps are used increasingly to provide measured doses of insulin for diabetics. In some hospitals, pain-suffering patients are being allowed to administer their own analgesic drugs through self-controlled external pumps. While patients in extreme pain show little risk of becoming addicted to morphine or other powerful painkillers that are administered by a nurse or doctor, it remains to be seen if this is true when the patient is in control.

Internal implanted pumps are being used to deliver controlled doses of anti-cancer drugs, either directly to the tumor or into the bloodstream. These hockey-puck-sized pumps are implanted under the skin in the patient's chest or abdomen; a smaller one is inserted under the scalp for treatment of disease in the central nervous system. One model contains two chambers: The first is filled with volatile liquid fluorocarbon, which is vaporized by the body's heat. The vaporized fluorocarbon expands and squeezes the second chamber, which contains the drug; the drug is thus forced into a catheter attached to a vein. Yet another drug-delivery model, powered by a battery, beeps when the patient needs more drug. It can also release drugs at different rates in response to remote control signals from a physician-operated radio transmitter.

MAKING MEDICINES

A whole new breed of drugs, conceived with hard-edged precision and mathematical foresight, has come about with the marriage of pharmacology and the microchip. Computerized molecular modeling first came to the fore of pharmacological research in the 1970s when the anti-ulcer drugs cimetidine and ranitidine were being developed. The traditional, plodding method of trial and error was being used, but researchers soon realized that these new drugs worked as a kind of molecular key that fit the ignition switch in the body cells responsible for the stomach's release of hydrochloric acid. Biochemists in laboratories worldwide began looking at cells as switches that could be turned on or off if the right key

OSMOTIC PILL

The osmotic pill cashes in on the scientific principle of osmosis, whereby water is drawn through a semi-permeable membrane from a medium with a high water concentration to a medium with a lower one. Drug in solid form is encased in membrane through which a microscopic hole has been drilled with a laser gun. After the pill is swallowed, water is drawn osmotically into the pill from the gastrointestinal tract. The water dissolves the drug, leading to controlled release of the drug solution through the laser-drilled hole.

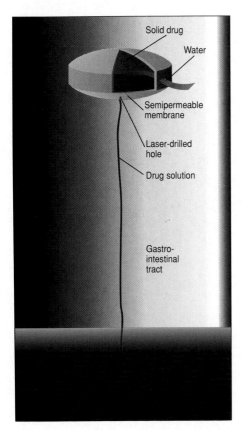

Solid drug

Water

Semipermeable membrane

Laser-drilled hole

Drug solution

Gastro-intestinal tract

Vitamin Mania

The human body needs a vast array of nutrients—including 23 essential vitamins and minerals—to fuel its biochemical systems, keep skin and organs healthy and protect itself from disease. A prolonged deficiency of vitamin C, for example, results in scurvy; victims experience general fatigue, inflamed gums, loose teeth and swollen joints. Yet the body itself is unable to manufacture important nutrients such as vitamin C; instead it must rely on an external source to supply them. It is possible to get all the nutrients included in the U.S. Food and Drug Administration's recommended daily allowance (RDA), listed in the chart at right, by following a well-rounded diet. Yet nearly 40 percent of Americans take a multiple or single vitamin and mineral supplement that often exceeds this recommendation. Opinion is divided on the benefits of excess vitamins.

Although supplements make sense for some—pregnant women and people following restrictive diets, for example—many others adhere to the old adage that more is better. And since a doctor's prescription is unnecessary for obtaining vitamins in the U.S., there is a risk of creating an imbalance in the body by self-prescribing an excessive amount of any one nutrient. Repeated daily doses of more than 500 milligrams of vitamin B6, taken to relieve premenstrual syndrome, can cause neurological damage, for example, and one-gram-per-day doses of vitamin C have resulted in "rebound" scurvy when the person abruptly stopped taking the megavitamin. Even vitamin E, touted by some people as a solution to the natural aging process and problems such as arthritis and infertility, has the potential to cause blood-thinning in some people. Although the RDA for vitamin E is 30 international units for adults, capsules that contain 1,000 IUs are sold.

Public opinion is divided on whether vitamin and mineral supplements are a curse or a cure. However, many doctors and nutritionists agree that the best source of nutrients is still a well-balanced diet. Megadoses, or any doses above the RDA, should only be taken in consultation with a physician.

A well-balanced diet, such as the meal illustrated here as vitamin and mineral tablets, will provide most people with the recommended daily allowance of nutrients.

THE VITAMIN AND MINERAL DAILY LINEUP

VITAMIN	U.S. RDA	NATURAL SOURCE
A (retinol)	5,000 IU (International units)	Liver, all milk, butter cheese, carrots, spinach and other green, leafy vegetables
B1 (thiamin)	1.5 mg (milligrams)	Yeast, rice, whole-grain breads and cereals, liver, pork, lean meats, poultry, eggs, fish, many fruits and vegetables
B2 (riboflavin)	1.7 mg	Dairy products, liver, yeast, fruits, whole-grain breads and cereals, lean meats, poultry
B3 (niacin)	20 mg	Liver, chicken, turkey, fish, milk, eggs, grains, fruits and vegetables
B6 (pyridoxine)	2.0 mg	Milk, liver, lean meats, whole-grain breads and cereals, vegetables
Folic acid	0.4 mg	Liver, many vegetables
Biotin	0.3 mg	Found in most foods
Pantothenic acid	10 mg	Eggs, liver, kidneys, peanuts, whole grains, most vegetables, fish
B12	6.0 micrograms	Liver, meat, eggs, milk
C (ascorbic acid)	60 mg	Broccoli, brussel sprouts, citrus fruits, tomatoes, potatoes, peppers, cabbage, many other fruits and vegetables
D (cholecalciferol)	400 IU	Fortified milk, fish-liver oils, sunlight on skin
E (tocopherol)	30 IU	Vegetable oils, whole grains, leafy vegetables

These U.S. daily allowance recommendations are for adults and children over the age of four.

existed. Theoretically, the right key in the right lock could control any one of the body's processes, from blood clotting to full-scale immune alert. Trial and error often led to undesired results—turning on the wrong process or producing no result at all because the "key" was not correct. Computer modeling eliminated the problems of trial and error, providing detailed computerized understanding of the cell's switch so that scientists could refine molecular keys for a more specific fit. This means greater pharmaceutical efficiency, including reduced side effects.

Computer modeling opens new possibilities for prevention, as well. Cold sores, for example, may soon be targeted by computer-designed vaccines. Researchers have discovered that the herpes 1 virus, which causes the unsightly nuisances, enters cells via a receptor site meant for a growth factor—a chemical that helps the cell develop; the virus wears a protein, Glycoprotein D, that is structurally similar to the growth factor. Computers are helping develop a dummy growth factor that would block the viral key and thus prevent infection.

Computers are only one resource of drug development. Many drugs are simply found readymade—in the human body, in the sea or in a plant. The chemical defenses used by plants and fungi to fight viruses and bacteria are a prime drug source. The contribution of the sea includes the anti-AIDS medication AZT, from herring sperm, and the antihypertensive drug eledone, from octopus saliva. The plant kingdom is a garden of pharmaceuticals, from humanity's oldest painkiller, the opium poppy, to purple foxglove, source of the heart drug digitalis. Animals, too, are a powerful source of drugs, an example of which is the hormone insulin, first extracted from a dog at the University of Toronto in 1921 by Drs. Frederick Banting and Charles Best.

Pharmacology owes an enormous debt to animal test models. Understanding of the brain's electrochemical communication, necessary before effective drugs can be developed, is based on studies of marine invertebrates such as the California sea hare. The Mexican salamander, axolotl, has the capacity of regenerating its heart muscles; pharmacologists are trying to isolate the responsible growth factor for application in the human heart. Scientists sometimes develop new strains to suit their purpose; the Watanabe rabbit, whose arteries are genetically programmed to clog up with cholesterol, is used to test drugs that break down lipids.

Serendipity lends a hand when drugs developed for one purpose turn out to have another application as well. Iproniazid, originally intended as an antituberculosis drug, was also discovered to have antidepressive effects; it has since been replaced by more effective antidepressants. Isotretinoin, a treatment for acne, may prove useful against throat cancer.

Perhaps the luckiest scientist in medical history was young Alexander Fleming, a bacteriologist in the germ lab at St. Mary's Hospital in London, England. During a microscopic examination of *Staphylococcus* bacteria in 1928, accidental exposure of the cultures resulted in some of the bacteria being killed by a mold. Although others had previously made the same observation, Fleming eventually turned his botched experiment into a medical miracle: penicillin.

Drug discovery and production, only loosely regulated in Fleming's day, continued in similarly unsupervised fashion until the early 1960s, when a wave of babies were born with deformed or stunted limbs, sometimes no limbs at all. A quick analysis of the reports revealed the common denominator: an over-the-

COMPUTER-ASSISTED DRUG DESIGN
The drug methotrexate—the white stick figure in this computer graphic—fights the spread of cancer by interfering with a key enzyme, shown as linked multicolored balls. The capacity of methotrexate to link with the enzyme—verifiable by computer—allows it to prevent cancer cell replication. The enzyme, which is necessary for DNA synthesis, naturally binds with a substance whose molecular structure resembles that of methotrexate. This similarity fools the enzyme into binding with the drug, and cell replication does not take place.

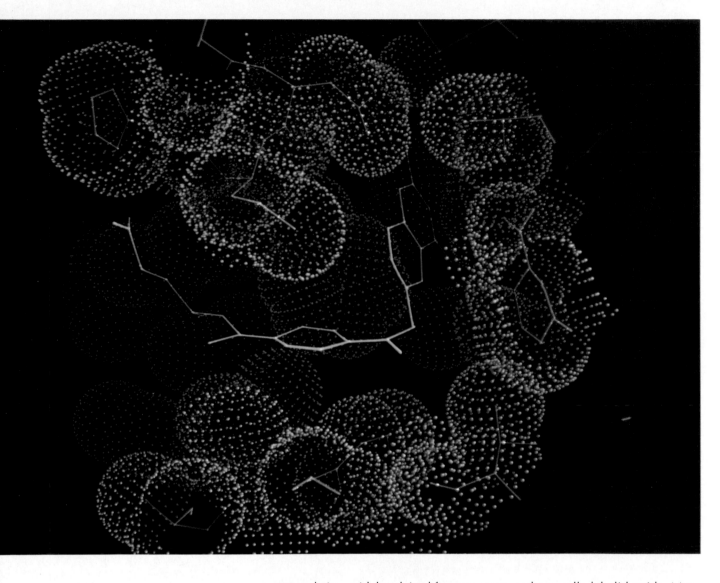

counter sedative, widely advised for expectant mothers, called thalidomide. Mentally normal, the approximately 10,000 "thalidomide babies" faced a life of handicaps and lawsuits. Thalidomide itself died an immediate death, leaving as its legacy drug laws that are draconian in their strictness. From test tube to patient, a decade of study and testing is now required before a new product is approved for human use. Development of the average new drug costs $65 million.

Toxicity testing begins with the lowest level of life and goes on up the evolutionary chain. Early in the process, tests on bacterial cultures weed out chemicals that induce inheritable mutations so that potentially dangerous drugs are not developed. The second stage is animal testing.

Initial animal studies are usually done on mice, along with at least one nonrodent, since results may differ from species to species. In early tests, animals are given repeated, massive doses of the drug. The aim is to find out, post mortem, what dose is toxic for 50 percent of test animals and which organs are damaged by overdose. Intermediate animal testing observes the effect of the candidate drug on fertility and general reproductive performance. Fetal abnormalities, as well as perinatal and postnatal toxicity, would raise red flags here. Meanwhile, in ongoing

Amazonia Pharmacopoeia

The prescribed bottles of tablets, capsules and syrups that line the shelves of a medicine cabinet seem far removed from Mother Nature—yet many drugs do have natural origins. The modern science of pharmacology relies, in large part, on the curative properties of plant and tree extracts used for centuries by indigenous peoples. Quinine, for instance—a remedy for malaria—is derived from the bark of the cinchona tree of Peru. And the rosy periwinkle plant from the tropical island of Madagascar contains chemical compounds that are effective in treating a number of cancers.

The world's tropical rain forests are home to plants that have yielded drugs used to treat snakebite, tetanus and even leukemia; an estimated 40 percent of drugs in use today were first derived from plant material. The planet's largest natural pharmacy is the rain forest of Amazonia, the largest portion of which is in Brazil. Its medicinal catalog, or pharmacopoeia, is relatively untapped; only a fraction of its plants have been documented. But researchers estimate that tropical forests will be destroyed within 20 years: Deforestation is ravaging about 150 acres per minute. Yet as new diseases appear, new drugs must be found or designed.

Ethnobotanists—scientists who study how tribal peoples administer the plants as medicine—are working against time to collect samples of plants. Working with tribal healers, they evaluate the pharmaceutical potential of the natural remedies; chemists then isolate the active chemical compound and analyze its molecular structure, hoping to discover the starting point from which to create new drugs.

Ethnobotanist Mark Plotkin, of Conservation International, learns the name and uses of an Amazonian plant from a Tirió Indian in Suriname. Less than one percent of the rain forests' plants have been investigated.

Skin secretions from this tropical frog, Dendro-bates pumilio, contain a substance that may be used to treat human cardiac failure.

chronic toxicity testing, a lower drug dose is administered over a longer period of time. The aim is to determine the chronic, long-term, toxic risk. It is during this final period that the cancer-causing potential can be measured.

Clinical—human—trials of most drugs follow three phases, each one longer and involving more test subjects than the last. During phase one, the drug is administered to healthy, paid volunteers—each having signed an informed consent form. Physicians study how the drug is distributed in, metabolized by and expelled from the human body, with a view to establishing dosage and detecting potentially harmful effects. As few as 20 volunteers participate in phase one trials, which last about a month.

Phase two clinical trials involve a few hundred unpaid volunteers who are suffering from the medical condition the drug is designed to treat. Over a span of several months, certain patients receive the test drug, while others are given the standard treatment. In what is called a double blind trial, neither patients nor doctors know who is getting what, neutralizing the effects of doctors' bias and patients' wishful thinking. If the drug is less efficient or produces more side effects than other test substances, it is unlikely to go on to phase three.

Phase three clinical trials help establish optimum doses and schedules, as well as to refine evidence on long-term safety. These tests may last three or four years, requiring the voluntary participation of thousands of patients and many medical centers, often in several countries. Even after the drug is marketed, regulatory boards continue to monitor performance.

On average, clinical trials take five years. Governing bodies such as the U.S. Food and Drug Administration usually require an additional two years to examine all data and license the new drug. The review committee must examine more than 100,000 pages of information, 80 percent of which has been generated from clinical trials. The ethical dilemma this procedure produces has been highlighted by the burgeoning of AIDS. Though taking an untested drug involves major risk, the 10 years required to bring a new drug to market could be a matter of life or death for an AIDS patient. The FDA is beginning to get around the problem. A program called IND—investigational new drugs—makes medication available to critically ill AIDS patients as soon as the phase one trials are completed.

Parallel tracking allows clinicians to carry on phase two and three testing while administering experimental drugs to patients who have the disease, but who do not qualify for standard clinical trials. This innovative approach is also being applied to patients with other incurable diseases, such as terminal cancer. Meanwhile, the ultimate fast track is the community trial, which entirely skips phases two and three of the clinical trials by dispensing new drugs to patients who serve as test subjects. Reserved for drugs considered good candidates in the treatment of terminal conditions, this system requires that potential pharmaceuticals undergo the usual rigorous scrutiny while allowing patients to benefit immediately from their curative properties; although community trials avoid the long wait for government approval, the patient is responsible for any potential risks. More than two dozen new AIDS drugs are currently being tested in such trials. In June, 1989,

The efficacy of antibacterial drugs is illustrated by this test in a petri dish of bacterial culture during an early stage of drug development. An effective drug will clear a circular area of the culture, as shown above, demonstrating its ability to kill bacteria. The size of the cleared area is relative to the drug's effectiveness.

one and a half years premature according to the standard time-frame, the anti-AIDS drug aerosolized pentamidine was the first medication to be approved by the FDA solely on the basis of community trials.

Nevertheless, even a drug that has been licensed for clinical use and sale remains vulnerable to governmental rejection. If pentamidine, say, suddenly were to demonstrate toxic properties, it would immediately be withdrawn from the market.

MANUFACTURING DRUGS

Even if all goes well, pharmaceutical manufacturing remains a high-risk business. When the developing company's patent expires—after 20 years in the U.S.—the drug enters public domain, leaving rival companies free to manufacture and market a generic copy. Likely to diminish the original investor's profit, this free market competition sometimes—though not always—benefits the consumer.

Manufacturing begins with the standardization of production methods: Every stage of chemical synthesis is scrutinized for safety and efficiency; all procedures are streamlined to cut costs and speed up the manufacturing process. The form in which a drug is manufactured depends both on the active ingredient and also upon the patients for whom it is targeted. While drugs for children are usually marketed in concentrated drops, most adults find it more convenient to pop a tablet than to fiddle with a spoon. Foul-tasting substances are made palatable in a sugary syrup, or spirited past the taste buds in a gelatin capsule. Medications that become unstable in the digestive system may have to be injected.

Sometimes the drug form that is most appropriate turns out to be a production nightmare. Most dermatological preparations are best delivered as ointments, for example, but the difficulty of controlling the absorption of a substance through the skin leads to endless trial and error experimentation. Liquid formulations are easy to take but tricky to make. Some drugs liquefy well enough, but then tend to revert to a crystal state, like the sugar crystals that can form in liquid honey. Others separate into their component parts, refusing to homogenize even when the bottle is shaken prior to consumption; the result could be a faulty dosage. One method of achieving uniform consistency and pharmaceutical character is to dis-

DRUG TESTING

Regulatory boards require drug manufacturers to submit new drugs to both animal and human, or clinical, trials. Animal testing, represented by the mauve arrows below, begins during the preclinical period, which can last from one to three years; short-term animal tests are used to determine the acute toxicity of a drug, whereas long-term tests are performed to investigate the drug's potential toxicity over a period of years. Tests on bacterial cultures may also be performed during the preclinical period. Human trials, represented here by peach-colored arrows, are conducted during the clinical period, which can last from two to ten years. These trials help determine the drugs appropriate dosage, its efficacy in treatment and its potential side effects.

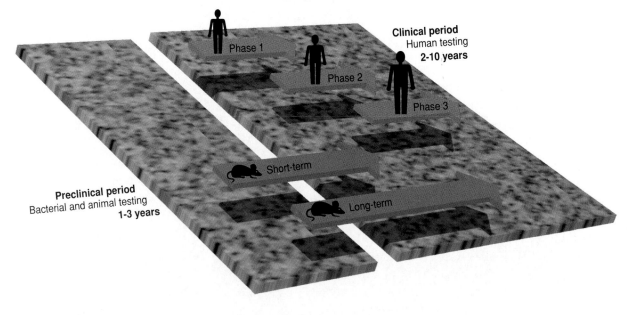

Phase 1

Clinical period
Human testing
2-10 years

Phase 2

Phase 3

Short-term

Long-term

Preclinical period
Bacterial and animal testing
1-3 years

solve drugs in a syrup. An elixir, or tonic, is made by first dissolving the drug either in alcohol or propylene glycol—a sweet viscous liquid—then mixing the compound with syrup.

In technical parlance, the word "pill" refers exclusively to something that is rolled, a process now only employed in Japan. Elsewhere, pills have been replaced by tablets and capsules. Tablet production may entail as many as 10 steps, including grinding components to fine powders; mixing the powders, usually with an inert binding substance; and compressing the powder with a steel punch. In order to mask a harsh taste or to protect the drug from the stomach's acidic juices, a coating is frequently sprayed on tablets. Capsule shells, on the other hand, are made of gelatin, then placed in tiny molds. A machine fills one half of the capsule body with a mixture of medication and an inert diluent, then caps it. Some machines can produce up to 125,000 capsules per hour.

Pharmaceutical engineering is constantly being improved. Advanced milling techniques have led to the production of ever-finer powders, rendering a drug more easily absorbable. Such minute particles facilitate the development of aerosol sprays for medications that must reach the respiratory tract, such as the asthma drug salbutamol, which is administered by an inhaler pump.

All drugs are manufactured in an extremely clean atmosphere, but sterility is the *sine qua non* for drugs that will be injected. Since the injected drug will bypass many of the body's defense mechanisms, it could inadvertently act as the perfect carrier for hitchhiking invaders. The working environment is kept pure by a series

Sterility reigns at a filling station for ampoules of drugs intended for injection (above). Unlike drugs to be administered orally or on the skin, drugs that are injected bypass many of the body's defenses; extra care must therefore be taken to avoid the potential injection of a harmful agent directly into the bloodstream. Meanwhile, at the end of a production line, an employee ensures quality control by examining each capsule on a light table (below); capsules that are misshapen, of an odd color, or suspicious in any way are removed.

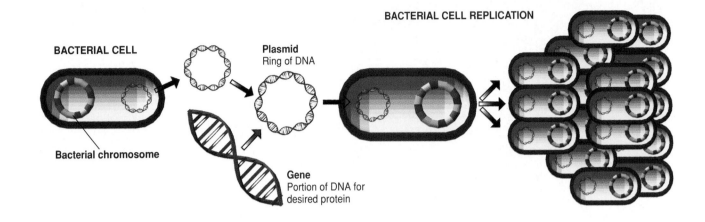

BACTERIAL CELL REPLICATION

BACTERIAL CELL

Bacterial chromosome

Plasmid
Ring of DNA

Gene
Portion of DNA for
desired protein

GENETIC ENGINEERING IN DRUG PRODUCTION

Drugs that are proteins, such as insulin, can be produced by genetic engineering, using the genetic machinery of bacterial cells. The composition of every protein is determined by genetic information carried in DNA. While the portion of genetic information that is vital for bacterial survival is contained in a cell structure called the chromosome, additional information is often contained in plasmids—small rings of DNA that are separate from the chromosome. The first step in genetic engineering is to select the responsible portion of DNA—or gene—that corresponds to the desired protein. Next, scientists splice this gene into a plasmid that has been removed from a bacterial cell. The plasmid is then inserted into a second bacterial cell. As the cell reproduces, the plasmid—including the desired gene—also replicates. Finally, the bacteria produce abundant quantities of the gene-encoded protein.

of air locks that keep out floating microorganisms, and the machines that fill the drug ampoules are bathed in germ-killing ultraviolet light. High-tech weigh scales and light sensors team up with eagle-eyed human monitors to maintain quality control. Each drug unit—capsule, tablet or ampoule—must contain identical quantities. Inaccurate measurement at any stage could lead to the ultimate error—underdosing or overdosing patients.

While many drug potions are stirred and mixed using some mechanized variation on the traditional vat and spoon, nature's own genetic machinery is being used to mass produce rare or hard-to-synthesize substances originating in the human body. Genes from human cells are spliced into the DNA of another type of cell—frequently a bacterium; this host cell then becomes a factory for manufacturing the proteins for which the inserted genes act as blueprints. Hormones and enzymes, important to human health, are now abundantly available thanks to such recombinant DNA technology, commonly known as genetic engineering.

Pharmaceutical insulin, still frequently extracted from the pancreases of cows or pigs, is apt to contain other undesirable substances. Today, actual human insulin—of the purest quality—can be manufactured through genetic engineering. So, too, with human growth hormone, prescribed to abnormally small children with a growth hormone defficiency. Tissue plasminogen activator, a human enzyme that helps dissolve blood clots, occurs in the body in minute quantities. Through genetic engineering, this enzyme is now produced in massive quantities; it has been shown to reduce the risk of death when administered within six hours of a heart attack. As well, immune system messenger chemicals, such as interferon and interleukin, are now widely available for experimental treatments.

The most common recombinant DNA factories are yeast cells, mammalian cells and bacteria, but plants, too, are being used experimentally. Ironically, tobacco is being engineered genetically to grow antibodies intended to combat lung cancer. Also in the experimental stage, rape plants are being used to manufacture enkephalins, one of the brain's natural painkillers, and the lowly potato is producing serum albumin, a blood protein used in transfusions.

Nine or ten thousand years ago the human race took a giant step towards partnership with nature by cultivating wild grasses and domesticating animals. Genetic drug engineering, harnessing natural processes to promote health and well-being, is a step of the same magnitude.

Panacea in a Pill

Hippocrates knew it, mother knew it, and so did the doctor who recommended taking two and calling in the morning: For many ailments, the best medicine is aspirin. Originally extracted from willow leaves and bark, this analgesic found use as a painkiller both in classical Greece and in pre-Columbian America. Now consumed at the rate of more than 123 billion tablets a year, aspirin is earning new glory as the world's number-one cure-all.

Investigating how one drug can treat everything from migraine headaches to rheumatoid arthritis and reduce the risk of strokes and heart attacks as well, researchers discovered that the secret lies in aspirin's chemical mechanism: The active ingredient, acetylsalicylic acid, interferes with the body's production of prostaglandins—hormone-like chemicals that are manufactured in great quantity in response to stress, such as a cut. First, prostaglandins sound an alarm by facilitating the transmission of pain signals to the brain. Second, they increase body temperature to fight infection and dilate blood vessels to allow extra blood into the area to augment healing. These tactics promote healing, but also cause the discomfort of pain, inflammation and fever. The sufferer may opt to take aspirin. Once absorbed into the body, acetylsalicylic acid goes to work, bonding with specific enzymes that act as catalysts for the production of prostaglandins, thus reducing the amount being made. The symptoms subside; a regulated aspirin dose ensures that healing continues, however.

Research shows that this tiny white pill can reduce heart attacks and strokes, both frequently caused by blood clots. Since prostaglandins play an essential role in the body's blood-clotting mechanism, many doctors prescribe a daily dose of aspirin to inhibit production of these chemicals.

Someday aspirin may even be incorporated into cancer chemotherapy regimens. Cells within a growing tumor release prostaglandins that form a protective barrier, prohibiting anticancer immune cells from attacking the cancerous cells. By inhibiting the effects of prostaglandins, aspirin may be able to reduce this barrier.

With scientists still discovering the benefits of aspirin, the old standby in the medicine cabinet is starting to look like a new drug.

These tablets work their magic because of their principal ingredient: acetylsalicylic acid, or ASA. The same substance, present in varying proportions, is the active ingredient in many cold medications.

Willow tree bark and leaves—sources of acetylsalicylic acid, the active ingredient of aspirin—have been used to treat aches and pains for centuries.

THE SURGICAL DOMAIN

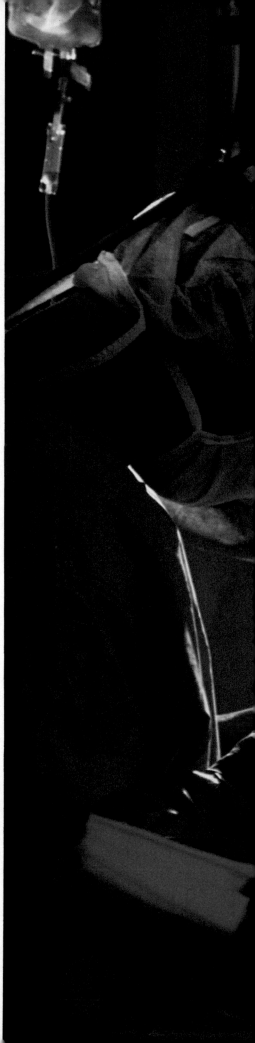

Most of Boston's surgical elite—voices hushed, attention riveted—stood in clusters in the circular operating theater at Massachusetts General Hospital. Their eminent colleague, Dr. John C. Warren, was about to perform. The operation, the surgical removal of a tumor from a patient's jaw, was a fairly routine procedure except for one momentous fact. For the first time in Warren's long career, his scalpel would inflict no pain. Just before the first cut, another man stepped forward. A former student of Warren's, Dr. William T.G. Morton was now a dentist, eager to demonstrate a new invention: a glass inhaler containing a sponge impregnated with ether. At Morton's instruction, the surgery patient breathed in the fumes. His face flushed, he twitched a bit, then he sank into unconsciousness. Morton turned to his old mentor and said, "Sir, your patient is ready."

So began a new age of surgical practice, in which a centuries-old heritage of agony and terror was replaced by the gentle sleep of anesthesia. Until that morning of October 16, 1846, surgery had been a brutish experience for all participants. Patients, subjected to excruciating pain, had to be strapped down to keep them from thrashing. Surgeons were forced to work at utmost speed in hopes of reducing the torture and minimizing the shock to their patients' systems. Even the most basic cuts and stitches became extremely difficult to execute when patients clenched their tissues at every move. Operations, consequently, were limited to rough, external procedures that could be done with dispatch—setting fractures, sewing up wounds and amputating limbs, for example.

All that had now changed. Thanks to Morton—and to other pioneers of the period who experimented with ether, nitrous oxide and chloroform—surgery moved into a new era of methodical control. Anesthesia bought time, allowing a surgeon to work with greater care, to refine his techniques and explore new procedures. As well as making surgery more pleasant, this innovation permitted whole new categories of operations, including cardiac surgery.

The members of this surgical team emanate discipline and concentration, even from behind their sterile masks. Precision governs every detail of operating room procedure, from standardized tool arrangement to traffic flow.

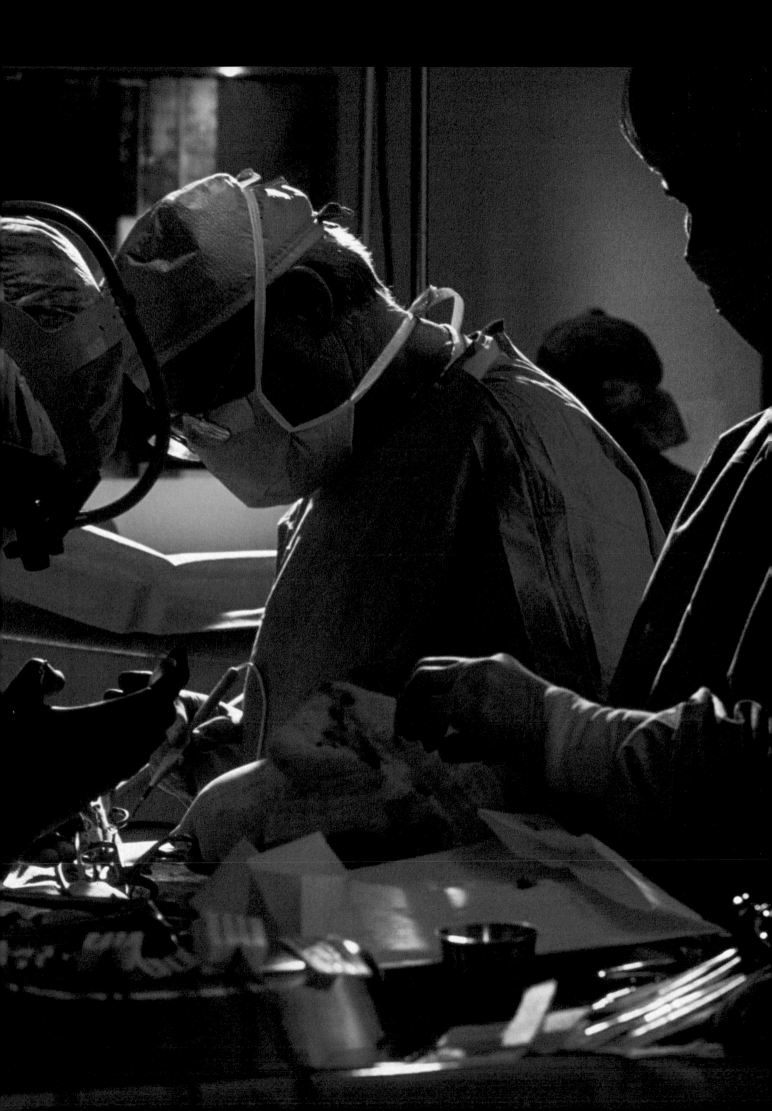

While one barrier to surgical success had been breached, there were still others. The worst danger in any surgical operation occurred not during the procedure itself, but afterward. More often than not, the patient would be hit with a severe postoperative infection, during which incisions formed pus and fever set in. And while the surgeon might justly pronounce the surgical procedure a complete success, he would have to admit that, alas, his patient had died. In the mid-1800s, 80 percent of all patients coming out of major surgery developed gangrene; an alarming number left the hospital directly for the morgue. Worse yet, no one really understood the reason why.

The man who changed this pattern, in 1867, was an Englishman named Joseph Lister, then chief surgeon at the Royal Infirmary in Glasgow. Casting about for a means of reducing the ghastly toll of postoperative infection at his hospital, Lister came upon a report by the French chemist Louis Pasteur, who recently had pinned down the source of biological infection. The culprit was a class of tiny, invisible organisms that Pasteur called microbes—the same microscopic agents that cause fruit to rot, beer to ferment and milk to sour. To Lister the solution seemed obvious: Kill the microbes.

Lister plunged his instruments in boiling water and used a powerful disinfectant known as carbolic acid to spray the operating room. The postoperative infection

Emergency!

A team of emergency medical technicians (EMTs) hops into an ambulance and speeds—lights flashing, siren wailing—to the scene of a car crash. On arrival, they will be required to act decisively, almost automatically, but never arbitrarily. Their task is to save lives.

Trained to respond to a vast range of emergency medical crises, ambulance attendants are called upon to deal with traffic accidents, heart attacks, drug overdose, major burns, suicide attempts—life-threatening situations that require lightning attention. Each emergency case is assessed as requiring either basic or advanced life support. Basic procedures are standard first aid, such as cardiopulmonary resuscitation—CPR—intermittent chest compression and mouth-to-mouth breathing, used to treat respiratory and cardiac arrest; advanced life support includes defibrillation—electrical stimulation to jumpstart a stopped heart—and administration of intravenous drugs.

Ambulances are equipped with specialized devices such as oxygen delivery apparatus and may even carry sophisticated tools such as electrocardiographs—used to record heart activity. Not the least important aid is the cellular phone, which facilitates communication with hospital personnel.

Though responsibilities and job titles vary between communities, some EMTs are authorized to administer drugs in cases such as asthma attack or diabetic coma.

Medicine on the road—or in the air, by helicopter—has evolved into a discipline that saves lives daily.

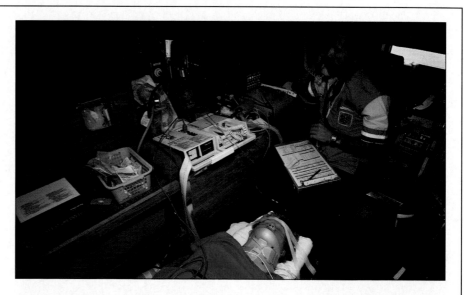

An ambulance technician radios ahead to the hospital, informing emergency physicians of the patient's status. A neck brace and bandages restrict the patient's head movement in case of neck or back injury, while a warm blanket prevents chill due to shock—decreased blood flow to vital organs. Speed of communication within the emergency medical system is essential. In the case of heart attack, CPR must be started within four minutes to prevent brain damage, and if defibrillation is used it must begin within 12 minutes.

rate plummeted and recoveries soared, making antisepsis the second cornerstone of modern surgical practice. Germ-fighting techniques have improved considerably since Lister's time, with the result that the surgeons of today operate in a virtually microbe-free environment.

Today, a third cornerstone is firmly in place. In previous centuries, even if a patient survived the surgery and escaped infection, loss of blood might still prove fatal. It was the leading cause of surgical fatality after infection. All kinds of methods were used to stem the flow, from the pressure of tourniquets to the use of red hot irons to cauterize open blood vessels. Now, not only has medicine learned how to replenish spilled blood by means of transfusions—the injection of blood from a healthy donor into the circulation of a patient—but surgeons can even command new varieties of high-tech scalpels that arrest bloodflow as they cut. Modern surgical operations resemble lightning-quick military strikes, where an aggressive and well-coordinated unit intervenes when other measures cannot solve the problem. At the head of the operating room team is the surgeon. Equipped with the knowledge and experience necessary to plan an appropriate course of action, and to modify that plan should unforeseen circumstances arise, the surgeon must invade the body benevolently, fix what is wrong as quickly as possible, and then pull out. But well before any surgery begins, the cloistered room within which it will take place must be prepared and cleansed of the lurking alien horde of microbes that can cause life-threatening infections.

ASEPTIC TECHNIQUE

Invisible to the naked eye, microbes may include bacteria, fungi, viruses, yeasts and molds. They can live with or without oxygen, and are omnipresent. They live in the air we breathe, the water we drink, the food we eat. They inhabit dust motes or "fomites" just as human beings colonize the Earth. Most dangerously, at least in the operating room environment, these potential invaders live on and within even the healthiest human being, invading hair, skin, body orifices and the intestinal tract in astronomical numbers. Consequently, reducing the presence of microbes to an absolute minimum in the operating room is mandatory, an ongoing battle that begins with the design of the working area and continues until the end of each surgical operation. Careful attention must be paid to the preoperative preparation of the patient, the surgical team, the instruments and monitoring equipment, and the operating room, or OR, itself. This multi-front, germicidal search-and-destroy mission is known as the aseptic technique.

A *sine qua non* of modern surgery, along with anesthesia and blood transfusion, asepsis is a prime criterion that is factored into the architectural design of all hospital operating theaters. Most big city hospitals build OR suites in modules separate from the general patient population, but close to critical care wards and service support facilities such as the pathology lab, X-ray department and blood bank. Connected to each other by short access corridors, the overall layout of suites usually follows a racetrack oval or rectangular pattern, and is subdivided into "semi-restricted" and "restricted" zones. These zones are intrinsic to aseptic technique, progressively isolating patients from unrestricted contact with the microbe-besieged people and materials of the everyday world. The semi-restricted zone, or outer circle, can be entered only by patients and hospital personnel wearing clean germ-resistant clothing known as scrub attire. This zone usually includes the short access corridors connecting the operating rooms, storage areas for clean unsterilized surgical instruments and, in some cases, glassed-off monitoring rooms, housing specialized equipment used during complicated operations.

The restricted zone, truly the inner sanctum of aseptic technique, includes all areas where the most stringent aseptic techniques are performed, and is limited to inside traffic. Here, everyone except the patient wears surgical masks and OR attire. Restricted zones usually include the operating room itself, a central scrub area for the surgical team, as well as a sub-sterile room, containing an autoclave—a device which uses steam heat under pressure to sterilize instruments and supplies. Chemical methods may also be used to sterilize surgical tools. The central sterile supply room, also located here, stores surgery-ready instruments, linens, sponges, gloves and other necessities such as sterile needles and sutures. Sterilized items are packaged in time-dated and germ-resistant wrappers. Supplies are carried to the OR by operating room personnel, or may reach the operating theater directly from the hospital's central processing department via a dumbwaiter, monorail, conveyor-belt, or on a specially designed and decontaminated "closed-vault" cart. Some fragile instruments and precious materials may never leave the operating room. They are used, cleaned, decontaminated and stored there.

Concomitant with this progressively aseptic isolation is the strict control of traffic patterns. The transport of clean and sterile supplies and equipment, for example, is distanced from the transport of waste and soiled items; once used, instruments and linen are removed from the clean core area for disposal. No soiled items must ever return to the clean area, preventing the contamination of sterile supplies, the patient and personnel.

Nowhere is the one-way separation of sterile from contaminated areas observed more strictly than within the confines of the OR proper. In fact, the first crucial member of the surgical team to arrive on the scene in a modern operating theater is neither surgeon, anesthesiologist nor operating room nurse. Gowned, capped, masked and latex-gloved, this essential player is a housekeeping attendant, armed with cleaning supplies and equipment. The housekeeping attendant's mission is to wash down and meticulously wipe dry all large vertical and horizontal surfaces in the operating room, including the floor, ceiling, walls, fixtures and lights.

Standard operating room design planning demands that it be constructed of nonporous materials; ceramic tiles are not used because the grouting offers a safe harbor for microbes, even when it has been well scrubbed. Ceiling, walls and floor thus present a seamless surface to maximize the efforts of the housecleaning staff not only to clean, but also to dry the operating room—water is a universal conduit for microbes. Storage cabinets, waste receptacles, explosion-proof electrical outlets, X-ray viewing boxes, and the various inlet valves for piped-in compressed air, vac-

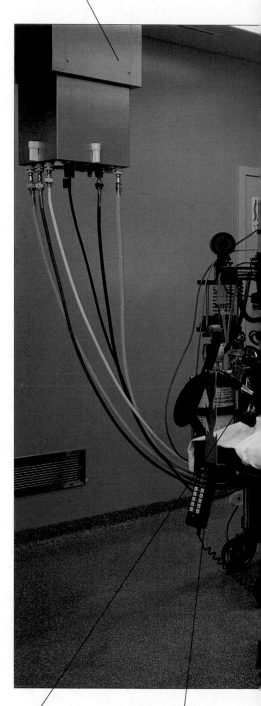

Anesthetic boom
Supplies suction and gases through color-coded tubes: yellow for vacuum, white for oxygen, blue for nitrous oxide gas and black for compressed air.

Mask
Delivers oxygen prior to administration of anesthesia.

Control panel
Adjusts the height and position of the operating table.

THE OPERATING ROOM

Few interior spaces are planned with the rigorous foresight devoted to operating room design. Here, more than anywhere, the patient is vulnerable to minute dangers: A delay of only seconds or the invasion of unseen bacteria could cost a life. Nothing is over looked in the creation of a sterile, efficient environment.

Oximeter
Measures blood oxygen level by assessing absorption of red and infrared light passed through patient's finger.

Electrocardiograph
Monitors electrical signals of heartbeat.

Spotlights
Provide intense illumination at operation site.

X-ray viewer
Illuminates X-ray films.

Time-elapsed clock
Indicates duration of procedure, starting at 0:00.

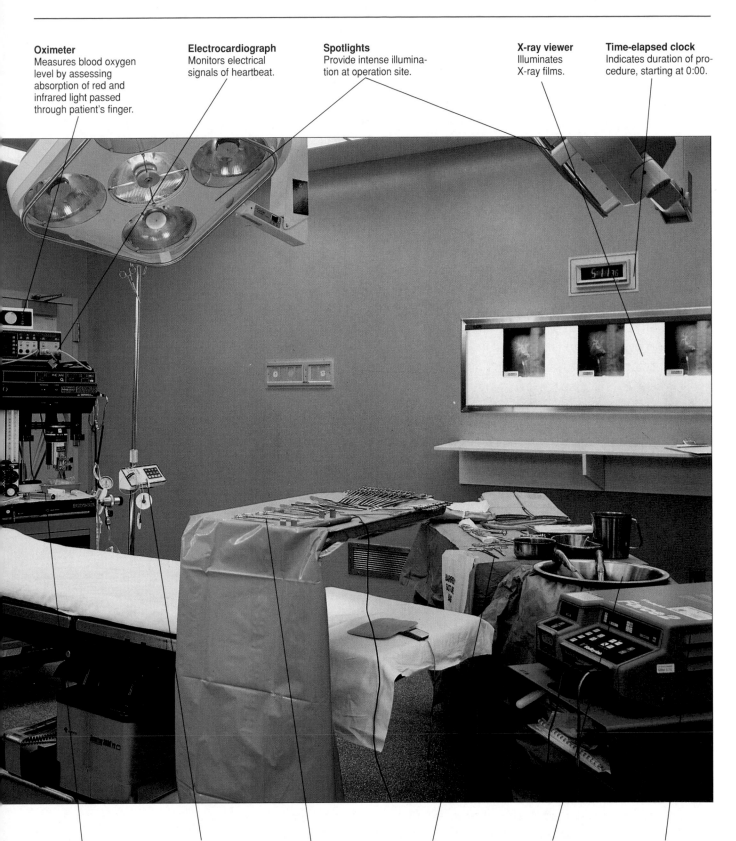

Anesthesia machine
Measures and dispenses anesthetic gases and vapors—the vaporized state of substances originating as liquids.

Peripheral nerve stimulator
Uses electric current to test muscle relaxation during anesthesia.

Mayo stand
Accommodates surgical instruments.

Case cart
Transports sterile drapes and instruments; also serves as basic table.

Ring stand with basin
Holds sterile water for rinsing surgical instruments and wetting compresses.

Electrosurgery equipment
Uses electrical heat to cauterize blood vessels and cut tissue.

uum suction, oxygen and anesthesia gases, are all recessed into the wall whenever possible, presenting no crevice in which microbes might hide.

Dust and airborne germs settle mostly on the floor and other horizontal surfaces of the operating room. The natural force of gravity is further enhanced by the room's high-flow, unidirectional ventilation system, which gently wafts air downward from ceiling-mounted inlet vents. Air is removed by exhaust ports at floor level and recycled through particulant filters capable of trapping more than 99 percent of all bacteria and most viruses. Considered an adjunct to aseptic technique, air-flow systems provide at least 25 complete exchanges of air per hour; in burn units, where the patient is extremely vulnerable to contamination, as many as 600 exchanges per hour are possible. Bacterial growth is further suppressed by climate controls, which keep air at 50 percent humidity and between 68-75° F. Because air-flow systems ensure that slightly more air enters than exits, a positive outward pressure prevents unfiltered, contaminated air from seeping in. Windows are rare in surgical suites; they are difficult to keep clean and the light they admit interferes with the precise illumination required for surgery.

At center stage is the operating table, equipped with attachments and armboards for supporting the patient in various positions, each determined by the surgical procedure to be performed. Placed just above and across the patient, but below the point of surgical incision, is the Mayo stand, a frame with a removable stainless steel tray, on which a succession of sterile surgical instruments will be placed as the operation progresses. Arranged nearby are small tables for backup instruments, sponges and other supplies, a ring stand for basins, the anesthesia machine and its equipment table, stands for intravenous bags, suction apparatus, and wheeled buckets for soiled linens and sponges.

THE STERILE FIELD

Absolute asepsis is maintained in what is called the sterile field, the area immediately surrounding the patient's incision—head, shoulders and arms are exempted to facilitate patient care. In order to prevent infection, the incision area is restricted to one division of the operating room team that has received a sterile scrubbing down—a distinction that is used to classify team members into two discrete groups. The "scrubbed, sterile" team consists of the operating surgeon, the surgeon's assistants and the scrub person—either a registered nurse or a surgical technologist. The "unscrubbed, unsterile" team is made up principally of the anesthesiologist and a registered nurse called the circulator, who assists the scrubbed team in a number of tasks, including replenishing supplies and labeling specimens. Only the team that has been scrubbed may work and handle sterile items within the sterile field; the unscrubbed team must function outside and around it, handling only supplies and equipment not considered sterile.

Before approaching the operating table, the scrubbed team members first wash their hands and arms in the scrub room, using a disposable brush or sponge and a powerful, rapid-acting, antimicrobial soap that leaves a germ-retardant residue on the skin for several hours. A sterile towel is used to dry fingers, hands and forearms. Although skin can never be rendered sterile, this protocol reduces microbes to an absolute minimum known as "surgically clean." A mask and a lint-free hat or hood covers head and facial hair to catch falling bacteria and dandruff.

A view of the surgical team is the patient's last image before succumbing to the deep sleep of general anesthesia. The core players are the surgeon, who performs the operation; the anesthesiologist, who keeps the patient unconscious, monitors vital signs and carries out blood transfusions; the scrub person, who passes instruments to the surgeon and watches for breaks in sterile technique; and the circulator who, along with other tasks such as assisting the anesthesiologist and keeping track of supplies, joins the scrub person in guarding the sterile field.

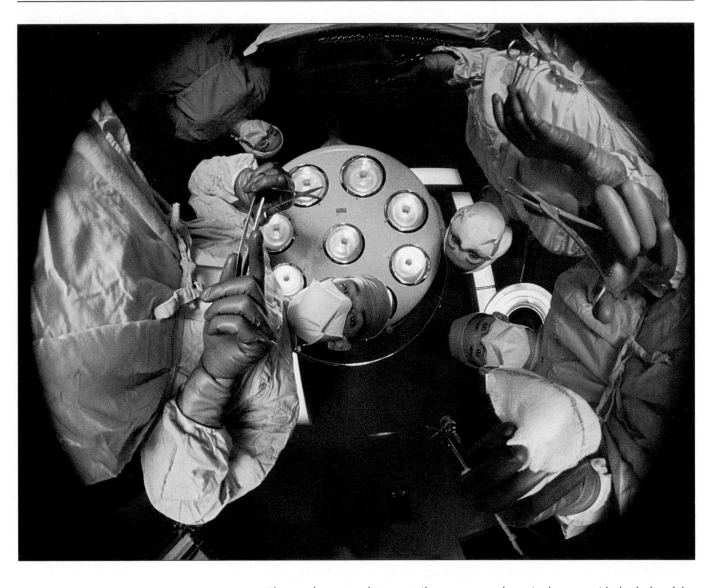

The scrub person dons a sterile wraparound surgical gown with the help of the circulator who, although considered unsterile, makes certain to touch only the inside of the scrub person's gown, thus maintaining the garment's outer sterility. After donning sterile and disposable surgical gloves, the scrub person helps the other scrubbed team members into their sterile gowns and gloves. Care is taken not to drag pant legs on the floor as they are pulled on. The suit top is tucked into the pants, and the pant bottoms are tucked into shoe covers. Face masks are exchanged for clean ones after each operation, and uniforms are changed anytime a team member leaves the restricted area. As well, operating room personnel are not allowed to wear jewelry of any kind, or even nail polish—germ-bearing flecks could chip off.

Next, the scrub person proceeds to the operating table and, along with the surgeon, employs an aseptic technique known as draping. Barriers to the passage of germs between unsterile and sterile areas, surgical drapes are made of non-tear, lint-free fabric that is antistatic and resistant to blood and aqueous fluids. Some drapes are disposable, while others are sterilized by steam under pressure. The scrub person drapes the operating table, the instrument tables, basins, the Mayo stand and the supply trays, then assembles an array of sterilized instruments on the draped tables. The patient is draped as well, leaving exposed the area of the planned surgical incision.

Given the elaborate aseptic measures inherent in overall OR design, and the steps taken by the sterile field team to be surgically clean, the greatest threat of incision infection during surgery comes from the patient's own body—specifically, from particles shed by the outer skin layer, the epidermis. All people continuously shed skin, much like trees shed leaves, and some, known as "shedders," drop decidedly more than others. The average person sheds between 4,000 and 10,000 skin particles per minute; shedders may disperse 30,000 per minute. Most of the dust in the average home, for instance, comes from its inhabitants; much of this dust, and the epidermal material it contains, is contaminated by virulent microbes—usually *Staphylococcus aureus*. Draping the patient contains this shedding, just as OR attire contains the surgical team's skin particles.

Before the operation begins, either the scrub person, the surgeon or a surgical assistant employs an alcohol-based disinfectant to clean the exposed site on the patient, who previously has been thoroughly bathed. During surgery, the responsibility for maintaining asepsis within the sterile field falls to the vigilance of the scrub person, who is charged with passing sterile instruments to the surgeon, and the unscrubbed circulator, who observes from outside the sterile boundary.

Mistakes can be subtle. After a sterile package or container is opened, for example, the edges must not be touched by a scrubbed member; the edge of a bottle cap is considered contaminated after the cap has been removed from the bottle. Gowns are considered sterile only from the waist to shoulder level in front, because only this area is within peripheral vision. If either the scrub person or the circulator sees any other part of a team member's gown merely brush against a sterile table or draped area, he or she must immediately inform the surgeon that the sterile field has been contaminated. The patient must be reprepared and the entire instrument table must be replaced.

As well as monitoring sterile technique and other tasks, it is also the circulator's job to assist the anesthesiologist throughout the operation.

ANESTHESIA

The anesthesiologist is the head of the unscrubbed team. If the surgeon uses anatomic knowledge and instruments to "fix" the patient, the anesthesiologist uses pharmacologic knowledge and machines to keep the patient alive. The best-known task of the anesthesiologist is to maintain the state of anesthesia—unconsciousness, muscle relaxation and freedom from pain. Yet this essential professional handles many other duties as well, including monitoring the patient's cardiovascular and respiratory status—assisting in their maintenance where necessary—as well as monitoring and administering blood products and fluids such as glucose or saline solution, and standing ready to deliver high intensity care for an patient who is unresponsive. It is the anesthesiologist who looks to patients' overall welfare during the surgical experience, as well as in the immediate postoperative period.

Depending on the site of surgery, the patient's state of health and the desires of the surgeon and the patient, the anesthesiologist may recommend regional or general anesthesia. Except for emergency cases, it is the anesthesiologist who decides when the patient is ready for surgery to begin. His assessment of the patient began well before the surgery when he reviewed the patient's chart and evaluated laboratory data, along with findings of electrocardiograms, chest X rays and other diagnostic tests. He already will have examined the patient for factors affecting access to the upper airway, since loose or missing teeth and inadequate support of the neck may pose significant risks. Systemic problems such as cardiovascular disease or hypertension are of major concern as anesthesia interferes with normal cardiovascular and respiratory function.

Whatever the option chosen, the anesthesiologist may order preoperative sedatives 60 to 90 minutes before the operation to reduce the patient's anxiety. Although adult patients receive no liquids or food for six hours before elective surgery, medications are often prescribed to neutralize gastric contents. This min-

Assembly-line surgery

Borrowing from Henry Ford's automotive assembly line, the Institute of Eye Microsurgery in Moscow is applying an innovative means of treating common vision disorders. Specialized surgeons perform only one step of each operation, permitting simultaneous work on eight patients, all of whom have the same disorder.

An example of one such team operation—devised by founder Dr. Svyatoslav Fyodorov—is a procedure to reshape the eyeballs of nearsighted patients. The procedure, known as radial keratotomy, requires that carefully planned incisions be made in the eyeball in such a way that the eye will assume a more efficacious shape as tissue heals. Involving five subprocedures of varying difficulty, the operation is performed by five different doctors; the patients travel from one surgeon to the next on a revolving assembly of gurneys while each of the surgeons remains in place.

The first surgeon uses computer calculations to map incision lines—depending on the needs of the individual eye. Employing a diamond-sapphire scalpel, the second surgeon makes radial cuts around the periphery of the cornea—the transparent part of the front of the eyeball—then the third surgeon makes cuts at the cornea's center. As the incisions at

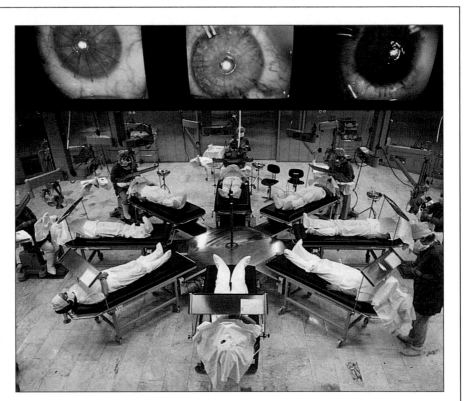

the center of the cornea are more demanding than those on the periphery, the third doctor—the leader of the team—is the most experienced of the five. A fourth surgeon verifies that the work of the others has been carried out correctly, while a fifth doctor washes the eyeball and injects antibiotics to discourage infection. Because the most experienced surgeons handle the most critical tasks—such as the delicate incisions to the center of the cornea—adherents to this approach claim improved quality control and reduced postoperative complications.

Eye surgeons work in assembly-line fashion at the Institute of Eye Microsurgery in Moscow to perform a radical cure for nearsightedness. As shown in video monitors *(above)*, radial incisions flatten the cornea, at the front of the eyeball, so that images focus precisely on the retina—a layer of light-sensitive cells lining the interior of the eye. As well as resulting in greater efficiency, the assembly-line system also permits a larger volume of eye surgery. The institute estimates that 250,000 eye operations will be carried out per year once its 12 satellite clinics are in place.

imizes the lung damage that can occur should the patient vomit and aspirate stomach acid during the operation.

General anesthesia has three phases: induction—from administration of anesthetic agents until surgery begins; maintenance—until near completion of surgery; and emergence from anesthesia. Induction begins as the patient is given pure oxygen by mask for two to three minutes. The goal is not only to "wash" gaseous nitrogen from the body, but also to supply the lungs with an oxygen reserve in case of respiratory dysfunction.

Next, a short-acting barbiturate—a drug which depresses central nervous system activity—is injected intravenously to induce unconsciousness. The patient, oblivious within 30 seconds, is then given a dose of muscle relaxant, which opens the throat, so that an endotracheal tube can be inserted for delivery of oxygen and anesthesia gases. The tube is equipped with an inflatable, doughnut-shaped cuff that is positioned one inch below the vocal cords, in order to seal the airway and hold the tube in place. Although researchers are not sure exactly how anesthesia works, it is believed that the transport of these agents to the brain produces pain-free unconsciousness by interfering with electrochemical nerve activity, both within the brain and among the peripheral nerves.

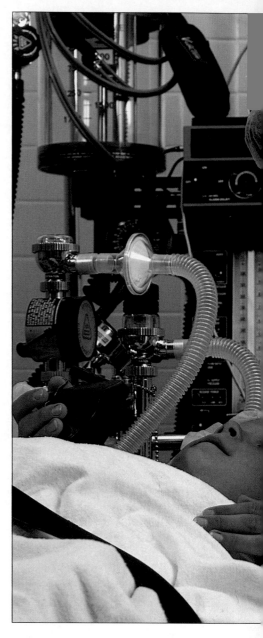

Maintenance of anesthesia during surgery is a delicate balancing act. The challenge is to conserve blood volume while balancing the delivery of intravenous drugs, inhalation gases, oxygen and muscle relaxants. By increasing or decreasing the concentration of general anesthetic in the patient's blood, anesthesiologists can speed up or slow down vital metabolic functions such as breathing and heart rate. At the same time, the "depth" of unconsciousness is fine-tuned to a specific level known as surgical anesthesia.

A variety of electronic monitors provides information to the anesthesiologist, who then uses this information in making decisions. In minor operations, the anesthesiologist may rely on relatively few monitors—showing, for example, blood pressure, cardiac activity and volume of breathing. Other instruments are frequently used to monitor blood oxygen level and to measure expired carbon dioxide, inspired oxygen and the concentration of anesthetic vapor in a sample from near the patient's mouth.

Following emergence from general anesthesia, the post-surgical patient is taken by the anesthesiologist and the circulator to the recovery area where the recovery room nurse and team are waiting to be briefed on the patient's status. Under orders from the anesthesiologist, recovery room nurses continue to monitor the patient's vital signs and carry out ongoing tasks such as the administration of medication and intravenous solutions.

Regional anesthesia blocks nerve conduction—transmission of messages from one nerve cell to another—in localized regions of the peripheral nervous system. A locally injected anesthetic agent stops nerve transmission in a prescribed area surrounding the site of the operation. A variation of this technique may be applied in cases involving healthy patients who are undergoing minor surgical procedures. Under these circumstances, a local anesthetic is administered to the surgical site, then it is supplemented with intravenous systemic drugs. These carefully measured injections not only dull pain and sedate, but also slow involuntary muscles, such as the heart, as well as glandular activity, all of which are controlled in some way by

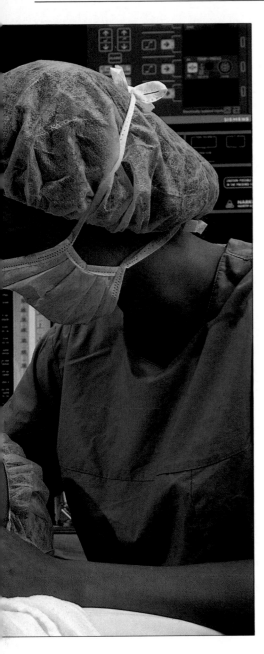

An anesthesiologist prepares to administer general anesthetic to a young patient. This is only one of the duties this professional will carry out during the course of the operation. After administration of the anesthetic—a combination of intravenous injection along with either gas or vapor—it is the anesthesiologist who decides at what moment surgery begins. Constant monitoring of the patient's physical state is also the role of the anesthesiologist, as is the postoperative follow-up.

the autonomic nervous system. Meanwhile, the anesthesiologist monitoring the patient's vital signs is ready to induce a general anesthesia immediately if it becomes necessary to do so.

BLOOD TRANSFUSION

The third pillar of modern surgery, blood transfusion, is also the responsibility of the anesthesiologist. Well in advance of operation day, an appropriate number of packed red blood cells and blood plasma units must be typed, cross-matched and stored. The body contains 11 to 12 pints of blood; during open heart surgery, in which the circulating blood takes a detour through a heart-lung machine, two to four pints of donor blood are commonly required to maintain levels.

Assisted by the circulator, the anesthesiologist monitors the patient's blood loss during the surgical operation. This is a difficult task, for while it is easy to quantify the amount of blood that enters the body, lost blood obviously is not extracted in measurable units. In order to arrive at a workable estimate, the circulator and anesthesiologist rely on two guides: an ongoing measurement of the volume of all fluids removed from the body by suction and a running tally of the number of surgical sponges used to control bleeding. Each sponge is counted and the sponges' overall weight is taken into account, providing a fairly accurate assessment of how much blood should be transfused to maintain a healthy balance.

Today's blood processing and transfusion techniques are built on the 1901 discovery of blood groups by Austrian-born American biologist Karl Landsteiner. He recognized that red blood cells bore substances, now known as antigens, that might cause clumping, or agglutination, if they encountered substances antagonistic to them in another person's red blood cells. Random transfusion could thus result in hemolytic transfusion reaction, a potentially lethal event. Landsteiner's obser-vation ultimately led him to identify three of the four major human blood groups—types A, B and O. The fourth, AB, was discovered by another research group a year later. Although surgical patients are given only transfusions of their own blood type, some cross-typing is possible in emergencies. Generally, individuals with type AB blood can receive all four blood types; people with type A blood can receive transfusions of types A and O; type Bs can receive types B and O; while those with type O can receive only type O transfusions.

In 1940, while conducting clumping reaction experiments on Rhesus monkeys, Landsteiner made another landmark discovery that led to the rhesus positive/rhesus negative blood group system, the other universal standard that enables safe blood transfusions. Donation of Rh positive blood to an Rh negative recipient could result in the formation of antibodies that would attack the donated red cells. Rh typing is especially important during pregnancy; antibodies formed in an Rh negative mother who is carrying an Rh positive fetus can lead to fetal death.

Modern blood typing procedures rest on Landsteiner's discoveries, using increasingly computer-automated chemical tests to assign donated blood to its correct group. Donor blood also is cross-matched routinely to test for patient compatibility. This test involves mixing samples of donor blood cells with a recipient's plasma—the straw-colored liquid that enables red and white blood cells to flow through the arteries and veins. If antibodies to the donor's blood appear in the recipient's plasma, the blood is deemed unsuitable for transfusion.

Since 1985, other increasingly sophisticated antibody tests have been used to screen donated blood for diseases such as syphilis, AIDS and hepatitis B. Further, a California-based genetic engineering firm has recently used gene-cloning techniques to test for the most common form of hepatitis spread by transfusions: viral hepatitis C—an inflammation of the liver. The test has become a standard disease filter in Canada, western Europe, Australia and Japan; it awaits FDA approval in the U.S., the land of its discovery.

Though they are powerful mass-screening tools, antibody tests do not recognize an actual virus, only antibodies to that virus. Antibodies are produced by white blood cells as part of an immune response to the virus, which is recognized as a foreign substance. The delay of this trigger-response process—about a week—poses a small but significant risk to transfusion recipients, since contaminated donor blood could be deemed free of viral contamination if screening tests were applied to it before antibody production had begun.

Recognizing this narrow window of vulnerability, a small percentage of elective surgery patients eliminate the possibility of receiving contaminated blood by "banking" their own blood during the five or six weeks prior to surgery. The time limit for blood storage is 35 days, because after that time red blood cells have a limited survival time in the patient. Barring a clerical error or contamination through mishandling, this process, called autologous transfusion, is perfectly safe. Unfortunately, some people are simply too anemic or weak to donate blood before surgery; donor-collected blood remains the norm.

The collection and preservation of donated blood is highly specialized. Today, less than 2 percent of transfused blood is given in whole form. Platelets and red and white blood cells are collected at the time of donation; the unwanted portions of the blood are returned to the donor. If whole blood is taken, laboratories use automated centrifuges to spin blood into its nearly 20 different components. Packed

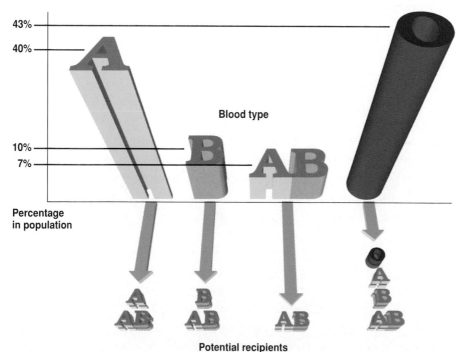

Blood type

Percentage in population

Potential recipients

BLOOD TYPING

Important to modern surgery, blood transfusion became possible with the discovery that there are four major human blood types: A, B, AB and O. Transfusions are generally blood-type specific, however other donor-recipient combinations are possible. People with type O blood—the most common—are called "universal donors," because their blood can usually be accepted by the other three types. Yet, while type Os are fortunate in their capacity to give, they are limited to receiving blood of their own kind. On the other hand, the rare individuals with type AB blood can receive blood of any type, but can only donate to other type ABs.

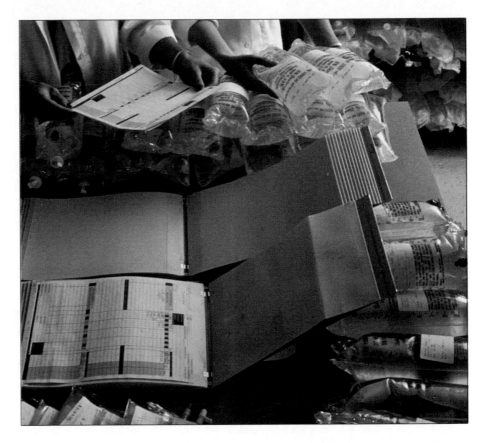

Blood bank technicians sort bags of plasma—the fluid remaining once blood cells have been removed—in a blood storage center. Behind-the-scenes preparation for blood transfusion requires that whole blood be filtered into its components: red and white cells, platelets—essential to arrest bleeding—as well as plasma and more than a dozen other blood factors. Computers are used to classify donor files.

red cells are used to maintain oxygen levels in tissue during surgeries that involve blood loss; platelets help control bleeding during and after the operation; plasma bolsters the patient's blood volume and provides clotting proteins to check blood loss. These components are stored in hospital banks in a variety of ways. Fresh plasma, for instance, is "quick-frozen" and kept at -112° F. for up to 12 months. Packed red cells can be refrigerated for 35 days at 39.2° F., or up to 10 years if cryopreserved, or frozen, in liquid nitrogen at -85° F.

REPAIRING THE BODY

Modern surgery, thanks to aseptic technique, anesthesia, blood management, the discovery of X rays and antibiotic drug therapy, considers no part of the human body off-limits. Every body cavity and organ system is now safely within reach of the surgeon's knife, and at an increasingly microscopic level.

Still, despite the manifold advances in the field over recent years, many of the basic tools and techniques of the surgeon's trade are similar to those used in the 19th Century. Surgeons continue to rely on scalpels and scissors—known as "sharps"—flexible tissue-holding forceps, hemostatic clamps to control bleeding, incision retractors, suturing materials and suction/absorption equipment. The main work is accomplished with stainless steel sharps and grasping instruments; retractors and suction/absorption devices hold back tissue and drain surrounding fluid.

A far cry from surgeons of old, who were traditionally barbers with some anatomical knowledge, today's specialists possess a high degree of knowledge and technical skill, enabling them to make rapid decisions and avert crises. But in order to carry out first-class work, the surgeon depends on assistants for such

CUTTING

Dissecting scissors
Resembling barber's tools, dissecting scissors are employed when a short, snipping motion is required. These instruments are applied in cutting a variety of tissue structures, including blood vessels.

Rongeur
Shaped like a pair of needle-nosed pliers, the rongeur combines lever-action and strong sharp edges to cut through hard tissue. A squeezing and pulling motion is used to remove bone fragments.

Scalpels
Used by the surgeon to make incisions, these knives maintain their keen edges and sterility with the attachment—at least once per operation—of a new disposable blade.

HOLDING

Rake-ended retractors
Wielded by assistants, retractors hold tissues to expose the surgical site. Rake-ended retractors are applied to resilient tissues. Some, such as the chest retractor *(top)*, can be locked in place.

BASIC SURGICAL INSTRUMENTS

Though surgery's most commonly relied-upon tools are now made of contemporary stainless steel and have become more refined since surgery's primitive beginnings, they have changed little in form and remain variations on instruments used to execute the four major procedures of traditional surgery. Cutting instruments, which include dissecting scissors, scalpels and rongeurs, come in a variety of sizes and degrees of sharpness. Grasping tools—clamps and forceps—are used to manipulate tissue, chiefly by moving or squeezing it, while the family of instruments known as retractors hold tissue structures in place, often for long periods of time, in order to expose the surgical site. Finally, once the surgical intervention has been completed, the incision is closed either with a variation of the traditional needle and thread or with a stapler, specially designed for joining tissue.

GRASPING

Clamps
Employing a scissor-type lever-action, clamps *(right)* have blunt ends—either curved or bent—that are useful in squeezing blood vessels shut and securing tissue structures.

Forceps
Resembling tweezers in form and function, these instruments allow the surgical assistant a finger-like dexterity, making them the principal tool used in the fine separation of tissues.

CLOSING

Incision stapler
Similar to a paper stapler, this machine is used to close the incision. Once healing is on its way, the stainless steel clips are removed.

Smooth-ended retractors
Used to hold delicate organs away from the surgical site, these instruments improve the surgeon's view of the working area. Little pressure is required to draw soft organs away from their natural position.

Suture material and tools
Used to stitch tissue flaps together, a kit composed of suture material, a needle-holder and a curved, swaged—threaded—needle closes incisions.

supporting tasks as holding and moving tissue and cleaning the surgical site. The first assistant—ideally another surgeon, but sometimes a resident, a surgical nurse or a surgical technologist—follow the surgeon's lead with appropriate responses. Typically, the first assistant clamps blood vessels after the surgeon locates them, adjusts incision retractors on request to improve the surgeon's view of the operative site and performs suturing or stapling of the incision at the end of the operation. The second assistant is usually a fledgling resident or medical student learning how the operation is performed, but may be a qualified nurse or a surgical technologist. Second assistants may simply hold amd maintain tension on a retractor the surgeon has placed in the incision, often for prolonged periods.

The scalpel becomes an extension of the surgeon's hand. For large general incisions, many surgeons balance the pivot point of the scalpel on their index finger, moving the arm downward as a unit from the shoulder, so that pressure from the weight of the arm makes the cut. Fine cuts—made with an up-and-down sawing action—are controlled by finger movements alone, with the scalpel held like a pencil and the heel of the hand resting on adjacent tissue for stability. To change direction, around the navel, for instance, the surgeon's body and arm turn as a unit, while keeping the scalpel blade perpendicular to the cut. Deep incisions require several knife strokes, cutting layer by layer.

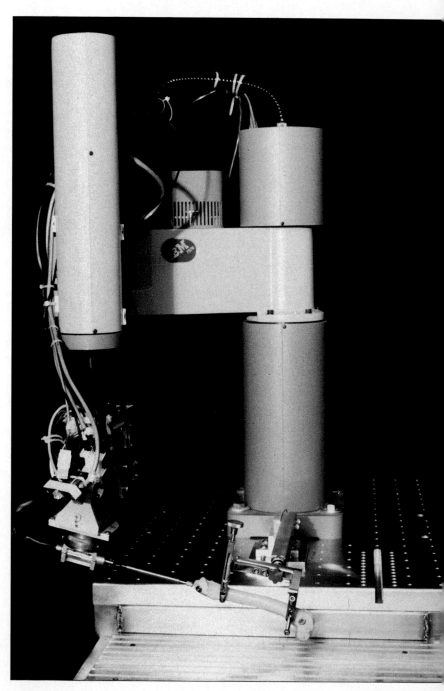

Part of the role of the first assistant is to pull on the tissue, spreading the incision as the surgeon makes successive cuts. Each sweep of the knife thus falls directly upon the cut that preceded it, resulting in a clean, vertically sheer incision rather than a terraced canyon effect.

While most scalpel cuts are made by drawing the blade towards the body, cuts using dissecting scissors move in the opposite direction—scissor cuts can be controlled by the natural rotation of forearm and wrist. Like scalpels, scissors are chosen for length, to keep the surgeon's hand outside the incision. Metzenbaum scissors—suitable for delicate tissues because of their sharp blades—are used for general dissection, while the heavier Mayo scissors serve to cut tough structures like tendons, and for bulk removal of dead tissues such as skin or muscle. Both are blunt-tipped to allow gentle spreading of incisions. Again, assistants use grasping and retracting tools to expose and stretch the tissue or structures taut, producing clean and smooth scissor cuts.

An experimental robotic arm, similar to those used in automobile assembly, is used in hip replacement surgery to drill a precisely mapped cavity in the thigh bone for implant attachment. Many hand-held instruments, for instance those used to excise brain tumors, may eventually be replaced by robotic arms with computer controls which can provide greater accuracy and stability than a surgeon's hand.

Among today's basic cutting tools is the electroscalpel, as familiar to the surgeon as the power saw is to a carpenter. Electrosurgery, whether performed on skin or deep tissues, is accomplished by sending pulses of high frequency electrical energy—about 600 kHz—to a small wire loop or needle that the surgeon wields like a scalpel. Used to destroy diseased tissue, make exact cuts and cauterize, electrosurgery eliminates the need for ligation—tying up blood vessels. Energy from the electroscalpel immediately causes the cells' water content to boil, making their membranes explode. The remnants of the membranes then stick together, resulting in hemostasis—cessation of bleeding. Cutting is achieved with almost no force, as tissues appear to melt away beneath the touch of the electroscalpel tip. Electroscalpels are often used in brain surgery, where an absolute requisite is microcoagulation of tiny vessels and the dexterous removal of diseased tissue without damage to neighboring areas.

Grasping instruments include a variety of forceps and clamps in various shapes and sizes, adapted to the tissues they are designed to hold. For instance, small forceps with multiple fine grasping teeth may be used to retract delicate tissue during dissection, or to hold the supporting structures of a nerve. Heavier-toothed versions are used to stabilize thicker flaps of skin during suturing.

Clamps hold blood vessels and intestinal structures for suturing—the closure of an incision. A long operation may require many small mosquito clamps to secure bleeding vessels while they are tied off with suture knots or stitched shut with a surgical needle. Vacuum suction tips evacuate escaped blood, while cotton napkins—called sponges because actual marine sponges once were used—are applied to dry the incision site.

Retractors—some hand-held by assistants, others self-retaining after they are set in place by the surgeon—expose the incision site to light and view. To avoid damaging healthy tissue, minimum force is applied. Tiny skin hooks are used for delicate work while rake retractors, resembling a bent fork, hold thick flaps of skin. Meanwhile, vein retractors, used to pull aside blood vessels and other cord-like structures, are the most commonly used hand-held retractors. Self-retaining versions, which are locked in place with ratchets or wingnuts, are harder on tissue, but leave the first assistant free for other tasks.

Incision closure can be carried out with a variety of suture materials. Most are fabricated from nonabsorbable substances such as silk, cotton, nylon, polyester, polypropylene or steel wire; as well, surgeons sometimes use absorbable catgut—actually made from the intestines of sheep. Completely absorbed by the body, catgut does not become a focus for microbial growth, making it useful in suturing cuts in the abdominal cavity if infection is present. Nonabsorbables, because they do remain intact, may act as transmission lines for microbes when used for internal or buried sutures, and are therefore avoided when the surgical site is known to be infected. Nonetheless, nonabsorbable sutures are applied internally in cases requiring sustained strength—steel sutures, for instance, are used to hold together severed tendons. All sutures come pre-sterilized in hermetically sealed packages, and are available in varying sizes. The thickness, length and tensile strength selected depend on the operation.

Suture needles, always held in a needle-gripping instrument, are curved in 1/4-circle, 3/8-circle, and 1/2-circle arcs, and are manufactured with either a cutting

Facial Reconstruction

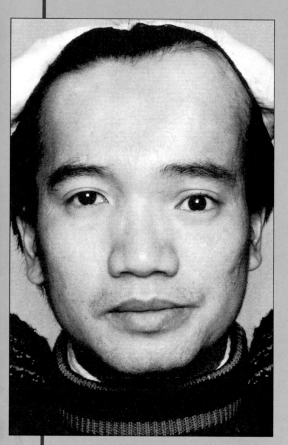

lastic surgery—the branch of medicine that deals with the reconstruction of deformed, disfigured or injured parts of the body—is often performed cosmetically solely to improve the appearance. In some operations, however, the face is literally re-formed by the surgeon.

Reconstructive plastic surgery, which mainly treats burns, accidental injury, and the correction of congenital defects such as hare-lip and cleft palate, grew out of surgical techniques that were used to treat injuries suffered by soldiers during the World Wars. Then in the late 1960s, a French doctor, Paul Tessier, demonstrated that large segments of the bones making up the face could be cut away and repositioned, and that the eyes could be moved horizontally or vertically without significantly affecting vision.

These two discoveries paved the way for delicate operations involving the participation of many specialists—plastic surgeons, neurosurgeons, ophthalmologists and dentists, among others. Preparation is painstaking and complex. Life-size photographs, X rays, CT scans—cross-sectional X rays—and computer-assisted three-dimensional images and models are all employed long before surgery begins. New products such as artificial bone and bone growth agents promise to expand the possibilities of the relatively young field of reconstructive surgery.

Thirty-one-year-old Jonathan suffers from a condition known as fibrous dysplasia, a rare disease in which normal bone is replaced by slowly growing abnormal bony tissue. The disease has created a prominent bump on his forehead and temple and pushed his left eye socket out and down.

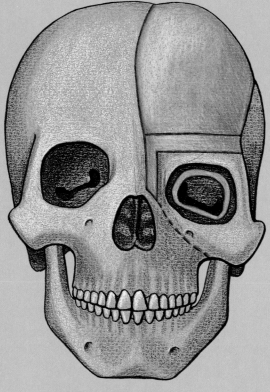

1. Before the operation
A sketch of Jonathan's skull prior to surgery shows the difference in eye levels. The blue areas indicate the amount of abnormal bone that needs to be removed and reconstructed; the dotted blue line shows where the socket bone should be cut.

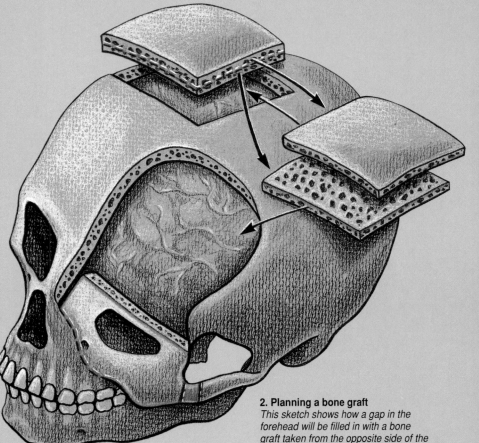

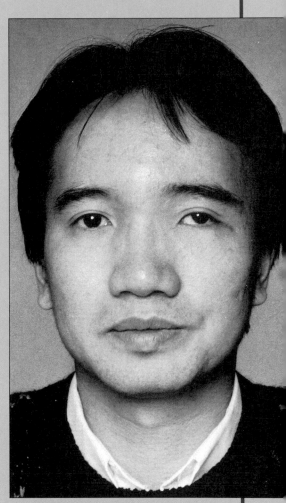

2. Planning a bone graft
This sketch shows how a gap in the forehead will be filled in with a bone graft taken from the opposite side of the skull. The bone cuts necessary to free the socket are identified by blue lines.

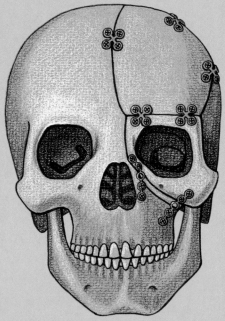

3. The result
After the operation, the eye socket is in its new position and the forehead has been reconstructed. The bone segments were joined with miniature titanium plates and screws.

Jonathan was discharged from the hospital 10 days after his 13-hour surgery. In spite of the postoperative swelling evident in this photograph, taken a few days after the surgery, the success of the complicated procedure is clear: Both eyes are level and the face is symmetrical.

edge—for piercing tough eye and skin tissues—or a tapered point, adapted to soft internal tissues. Some needles are equipped with eyes, but far more popular are swaged needles, to which sutures are permanently attached. The needle may finally be cut from the suture with scissors or, in semi-swaged versions, snapped free by the surgeon with a quick vertical tug of the needle holder.

To close arteries, veins, nerves and other small structures—especially if speed is required—surgeons may use small ligating clips instead of sutures. Set in place with a specialized tool, clips provide permanent closure of major vessels in hard-to-reach areas. Staple guns are also used in thoracic, abdominal, and gynecological surgery, especially for ligation, skin closure and anastomoses—rejoining severed tubular structures such as intestine or arteries. Because the tiny stainless steel staples have the standard B-shape of office staples when they are closed, nutrients are able to pass freely to the cut edges of the joined tissues, promoting healing.

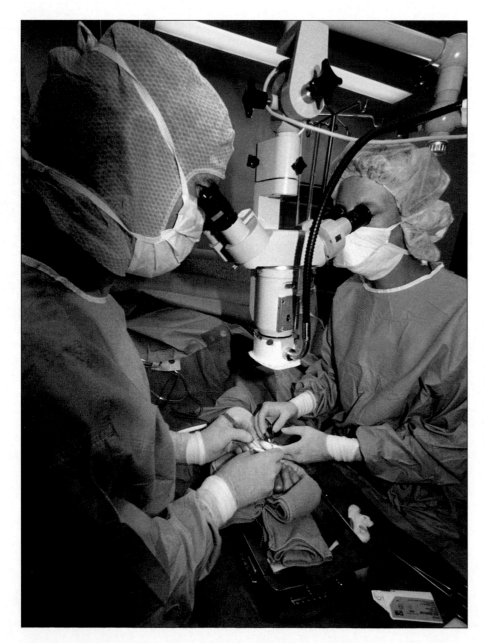

Working in tandem, two surgeons rely on the magnification of a double-headed operating microscope to see and mend tiny severed blood vessels and nerves in a damaged hand. Such delicate repair work, called microsurgery, is performed with miniaturized versions of standard surgical tools.

Doctors performing microsurgeries may soon rely on "people glue" rather than traditional sutures. Already being used experimentally, this "glue" enlists fibrinogen—a clotting protein found in blood plasma—to hold extremely small tissue structures in place while they heal.

The future of surgery in general appears headed toward the microcosmic frontiers of science. Since the double-headed operating microscope was first applied to the eye and inner ear in the mid-1950s, the field of microsurgery has addressed itself to ever more minute operative fields.

Executed on surgical sites less than half an inch across, microsurgical procedures are literally impossible to perform with the naked eye. While full-scale surgical techniques are executed with the wrist, hand and forearm, microsurgical cuts are basically scaled-down versions of the same maneuvers, performed solely by manipulating the fingers.

What is radically different, of course, is that the microsurgeon and the first assistant must rely on sight provided by microscope. The operating microscope is equipped with two eyepieces, revealing to both doctors a new plane of anatomical reality. Color filters increase light contrast, while graduated lenses provide small-step magnification powers of 6, 10, 16, 25, and 40 times the capacity of the naked eye. In this world, doctors are able to rejoin severed nerves, veins and arteries smaller in diameter than a human hair. The swaged needles they employ are 1/5,000 of an inch in diameter—the size of a single sliver of fiberglass.

Armed with such control over the minuscule, microsurgeons began reimplanting severed limbs in 1962, when a surgical team at Massachusetts General Hospital successfully rejoined the right arm of a 12-year-old boy. That historic operation led the way to other successful reimplantations: amputated fingers, toes, hands, even noses. Almost every body part has at one point been replaced on accident victims. More than once, a big toe has been reimplanted on an injured hand to replace an amputated thumb, and even an amputated penis has been reattached, complete with nerves and blood vessels intact.

Now, microsurgeons are trying to help childless couples have babies, with the aid of an artificial insemination technique that uses computer-guided robotic arms. The arms are equipped with a microneedle and a .002-inch-wide suction tube. The suction tube is used to grasp and steady a female egg—which is only about the size of a pinhole—so that the microneedle can drill a hole through the tough outer protein coat that surrounds it. Researchers hope this "tunnel of love" will provide an access route for the slow-moving sperm of men with low sperm counts.

Meanwhile, surgical technique continues to develop all across the board. A breakthrough in one discipline often sparks an astonishing advance in another.

BLOODLESS SURGERY

In the 1950s, the introduction of fiber optics enabled a whole range of therapeutic applications of the endoscope—a device for peering inside the body. The new bundles of optical fibers—usually hair-thin glass—transmitted light without heat, and they could bend and direct light in any direction. Not only did the development of fiber optics open a new world of diagnostic potential, it also made possible endoscopic surgery: probing deeply to carry out procedures that earlier would

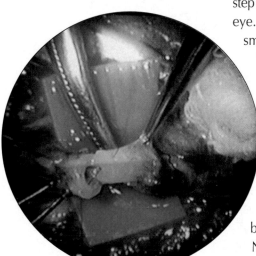

The reopening of a sperm duct, during reverse vasectomy, is viewed through the magnifying operating microscope and displayed on a TV monitor. Such exposure of the site of action enables the entire surgical team to participate in the procedure.

have meant cutting through skin, muscle and often bone.

To perform such surgery, a TV monitor or a surgical microscope is connected to a pencil-thin cable of optical fiber bundles. This enables the surgeon to view any spot where the cable can travel. A linked pair of thin tubes provide air and water, making it possible to irrigate, evacuate and dry the surgical site. Small, remote-controlled instruments, which may include probes, knives, scissors, forceps, curettes and cauterizing devices, are introduced through a fourth cable to make the repair. Today, endoscopy is one of surgery's technological superstars.

Arthroscopy, a form of elective surgery involving joints, is used with increasing frequency to treat professional athletes. While traditional techniques require major incisions to expose the operative site, arthroscopy usually requires one or more holes, each less than a half inch across. Postoperative recovery time of many operations has dropped from months to a couple of weeks. Widely used for orthopedic conditions, particularly those involving the shoulder and knee, arthroscopy effectively removes dead and damaged tissue from joints, as well as retrieving bone biopsies and performing partial removal or repair of torn menisci—the shock-absorbing cartilage that separates the knee cap from the knee joint.

In other applications, such as treatment of upper gastrointestinal tract disorders, a flexible endoscopic cable is swallowed by the patient after local anesthetic has been applied to the pharynx. Colonoscopy is now considered a gold standard procedure for the diagnosis and removal of precancerous polyps in the large intestine. It is performed by passing the fiber optic cable, with its enclosed grasping and excision instruments, into the rectum and up through the colon—as far as its juncture with the small intestine, if need be. Similar techniques are used in cystoscopy, to remove stones from all levels of the urogenital tract and to remove tumors in the bladder or a diseased prostate. Laparoscopy is used in an analogous way by gynecologists to recover eggs for in vitro fertilization.

Endoscopes are also being used as an adjunct to cryosurgical probes—ultracold knives that, like the electroscalpels frequently employed to cauterize blood vessels, exploit the high water content of cells. Cryosurgery takes the opposite tack from the heat of electrosurgery, using extreme cold to kill diseased skin and internal tissues. Direct or indirect application of liquid nitrogen at -320.8° Fahrenheit, or nitrous oxide at -129.1° Fahrenheit, causes near-instant crystallization of the water within a cell. The resultant ice "spikes" destroy the cell by piercing its outer membrane. The freezing also shuts down microcirculation to the cells; without a blood supply, they soon die from oxygen deprivation.

Dermatologists commonly apply cryogenic agents directly on the skin to destroy warts, precancerous moles and superficial cancers endemic to sunbathers. Cryo-

The blue-green beam of an argon gas laser shoots through the cornea and the lens of an animal's eye in a lab test to demonstrate how lasers are used to stop leaking blood vessels behind the cornea. The extreme heat of laser light is not absorbed in the bloodless cornea or lens so has no effect there. Since all colors are neutralized by their spectral opposites, however, the blue-green beam ceases traveling when it hits the red of the leaking blood; its heat is absorbed, welding the leaks.

gens may also be used in probes which have a heat exchange surface at the tip. At the contact area between probe tip and tissue, liquid cryogen turns to a gas and the heat transfer results in tissue cooling. In combination with an endoscope, the technique is commonly used to destroy internal genital warts and precancerous tissues of the cervix and prostate.

The efficiency and cost-effectiveness of cryosurgery have assured it a place in modern surgery. In recent years, however, its technological development and progress has slowed, due primarily to competition from a more powerful space-age tool—the laser.

CUTTING WITH LIGHT

Elegant in concept and effect, lasers represent modern surgery's ultimate cutting edge; every major surgical specialty employs this technique in some form. Using the energy of atoms, lasers cut with pure light. While powerful enough to vaporize a diamond, laser light is also exquisitely precise—an accomplished surgeon can laser-autograph a raw egg without breaking the yolk.

All lasers rely on a principle first postulated by Albert Einstein in 1917. If electrical energy is used to excite the atoms of a pure solid, liquid or gas, the charge will boost the orbit of the atoms' electrons—minuscule particles that revolve around the nucleus, or center, of the atom. The electrons' increased spin sends them orbiting farther away from the nucleus. But the moment the external energy source is interrupted, the natural electromagnetic pull of the nucleus sends the electrons back into their original orbits. At that instant, they shed any excess energy as tiny packets of light called photons.

The pure substance whose atoms are electrically excited in surgical lasers is gas. In a gas laser, the photons are captured in a long tube with mirrors at both ends. One mirror has only a semi-silver backing; while its surface has fair reflective properties, light of sufficient energy can pass through it. Photons bounce back and forth between these mirrors, amplifying their energy. Finally they become strong enough to leap through the semi-silver-backed mirror in the form of an almost pure beam of electromagnetic radiation. The acronym LASER stands for Light Amplification by Stimulated Emission of Radiation.

Unlike normal light, which is omnidirectional, laser photons all move in exactly the same direction, almost perfectly parallel to each other. Focused with a lens, they can pinpoint a target as small as one micron—approximately 0.00004 inches—across. The beam provokes a microexplosion that instantly vaporizes the target tissue, at the same time cauterizing blood vessels—again, making a bloodless cut. Since nothing but light touches the tissue, the laser beam is frictionless. Further, by channeling the laser through a fiber optic cable, the cutting beam can be conveyed into remote regions of the anatomy under local anesthetic.

Laser's color is helpful in aiming surgical cuts. Depending on which pure gas is subjected to an electrical charge, the resultant photon beams will have a specific color or wavelength: The excited carbon and oxygen atoms of carbon dioxide, for instance, give off red light; argon gas photons glow blue-green.

First used in eye surgery during the 1960s to spot-weld detached retinas back in place, modern surgical lasers are now used for everything from blasting plaque out of clogged arteries to zapping kidney stones. They have sculpted misshapen

Auto-syphgmomanometer
Measures the patient's blood pressure; a cuff, placed around the patient's upper arm automatically inflates and deflates and is connected to a device which records the blood pressure.

Cardiac monitor
Monitors the electrical activity of the heart; electrodes attached to the body, send electrical signals along wires to the recording machine which displays an image of the heart's activity during every heartbeat.

IV pump
Delivers medication, nutrients or fluid replacement through a needle placed in a patient's vein; an intravenous drip maintains a steady supply to the patient's bloodstream.

Defibrillator
Delivers a strong electrical shock to a heart that has stopped beating; two paddles connected to an external energy source send a 250-volt charge to the heart muscle.

Ventilator and endotracheal tubing
Provides a continuous supply of oxygen to a patient who is unable breathe on his own through a mouthpiece and a tube placed in the patient's trachea.

98

Critical Care

External pacemaker
Electrical impulses, generated by an external energy source, are introduced to the heart via electrodes; they cause the heart to beat with a regular rhythm.

Hypo-hyperthermy machine
Delivers heat or cold, to treat victims of hypothermia or high fever, by a pad placed under the patient.

Oximeter
Monitors blood oxygen level; a device slipped around the patient's finger sends infrared and red light through the finger and detects the amount of light that passes through the digit. This instrument is used in conjunction with a ventilator to ensure that there is sufficient oxygen in the blood.

Florence Nightingale, the founder of nursing, wrote in 1863: "It is not uncommon, in small country hospitals, to have a recess or small room leading from the operating theater in which the patients remain until they have recovered, or at least, recover from the immediate effects of the operation." Today, these alcoves have grown into specialized medical facilities called intensive care units, all designed, equipped and staffed to deal with life-threatening situations.

A general intensive care unit—ICU—provides vigilant around-the-clock observation of all critically ill patients in the hospital. These units are designed so that staff can observe all patients from a central location; often the patients' cubicles radiate from a central nurses' station. Some ICU devices, such as intravenous poles, automatic sphygmomanometers, cardiac monitors, suction apparatus and ventilators, are found at each patient's bedside, conveniently positioned for the constant demand; supplies, specialized equipment and drugs are contained in a crash cart which is kept in a central location and is available within seconds when an emergency strikes.

Some intensive care units, located adjacent to an operating theater, specialize in caring for postoperative patients. These units contain machines that monitor continuously the vital signs—such as heart rate, blood pressure and breathing regularity—of patients who are at high risk for airway obstruction, blood loss and shock caused by an inadequate supply of blood to the tissues.

Many large hospitals are also equipped with ICUs that specialize in caring for patients who suffer from similar ailments. Other specialized ICUs include shock and burn units, neonatal, neurosurgical, and acute respiratory units.

A multipurpose intensive care, unit—ICU—like the one shown here, is commonly found in small hospitals. These modern ICUs are dominated by high-tech equipment to monitor critically ill patients continuously.

corneas, excised tonsils and hemorrhoids, removed freckles and erased the red facial birthmarks known as port-wine stains.

Researchers are particularly interested in controlling the heat produced by the beams, and the depth to which they penetrate tissues. Carbon dioxide lasers create enough heat to vaporize cell water instantly, but at the same time, they sear adjacent tissues. Yttrium-aluminum-garnet—or YAG—lasers are sometimes used to "cook" rather than cut, turning tumors into coagulated lumps of easily removed debris. Excimer lasers, still in the developmental stage, use a cool light beam that shows promise in the removal of arterial plaque without burning through the wall of the vessel, and for correcting myopia—near-sightedness—by deftly sculpting the cornea without damaging nearby cells.

Laser light has been used for some time by a handful of the world's top genetic scientists as a scalpel or drill to pierce the outer membrane of cells, facilitating the insertion of new genes—collections of coded instructions that govern cell activity. In 1989, a cell biophysicist at the University of California at Irvine found a new way to use laser light—as both a drill and a forceps, holding two cells in place

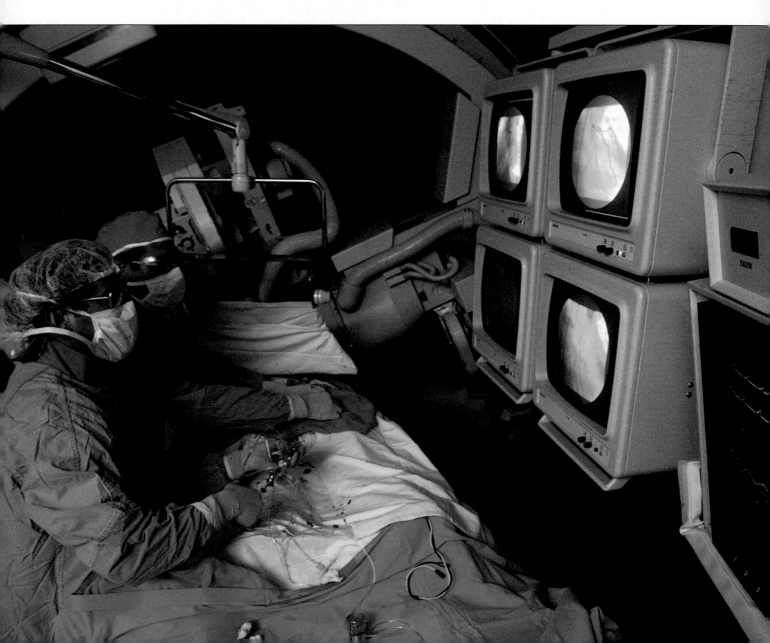

while he fused them. Now, inspired by microsurgical artificial insemination techniques, he plans an *in vitro* fertilization experiment to help handicapped sperm through the protein coat of the egg. But instead of cutting a hole through the cell's coat with robotic arms and microneedles—as in microsurgery—he will use the laser drill-and-forceps method.

Impressive as they are, lasers are merely surgery's sharpest instrument, not its final evolution. Beyond the bloodless knife, some techniques use no knife at all.

BALLOON SURGERY

Modern heart surgery, for instance, replaces the major coronary intervention traditionally employed to treat plaque-clogged arteries with a less traumatic technique using tiny balloons. A number of factors can contribute to a dangerous buildup of plaque in the coronary arteries—the blood vessels charged with supplying the heart with oxygen-rich blood from the lungs. As the clogged vessels grow narrower and less elastic, the individual can develop a vascular condition known as atherosclerosis. If the blockage worsens to the point where the heart becomes starved for oxygen, a condition known as angina pectoris sets in, marked by chest pains and shortness of breath. Severe blockage can cause a piece of the heart to suffocate and die from oxygen deprivation—heart attack—often the final stop along a degenerative road called coronary heart disease or CHD.

CHD accounts for 80 percent of all cardiac deaths, and is the leading cause of death among all western nations. For some time, scientists have known of the triggers associated with CHD—high blood cholesterol, fatty diets, obesity, smoking, hypertension little exercise and stress—but no one can yet explain how those factors actually translate into plaque formation. Mounds of yellowish tissue, composed of cells, connective tissue and lipids, or fat, accumulate just beneath the smooth inner lining, or intima, of a blood vessel wall. There, the material grows like a benign tumor, slowly protruding into the artery. Some scientists think excess blood cholesterol is the main culprit, infiltrating the intima and then gathering smooth muscle cells, lipids and calcium to itself; others say plaque results from an injury to the inner wall, caused by high blood pressure or tobacco smoke gases deposited in the blood.

While the debate continues, scientists do agree that plaque may lead to a heart attack; preventing this crisis is the goal of coronary artery surgery. Until recently, the prevailing method to accomplish this goal was coronary bypass surgery, a major operation involving general anesthesia, the opening of the chest wall and, finally, the graft of a healthy section of blood vessel from the patient's leg to replace the clogged section of coronary artery. Today, the preferred method is a procedure called percutaneous balloon angioplasty.

Considered almost noninvasive by comparison with a brutal operation such as the bypass, angioplasty is performed while patients are awake and mildly sedated. While monitoring the coronary artery site on a specialized X-ray machine called an angioscope, cardiologists gently feed a hollow catheter up through the femoral artery of the leg until it reaches the narrowed plaque site, or stenosis. A smaller catheter, with a small balloon at its tip, is then loaded into the hollow catheter. When it reaches the stenosis, the balloon is inflated with liquid, and its bulk compresses the plaque against the arterial walls.

Doctors, aided by a live X-ray image, guide an inch-long deflated balloon into a clogged coronary artery through a catheter. Once in position, the balloon is inflated, and clogging fatty material is pushed to the sides of the artery, clearing the way for less impeded blood flow. The procedure, called coronary angioplasty, is a relatively simple, inexpensive and safe alternative to the more risky coronary bypass operation.

Based on angioplasty's success rate, a similar balloon technique called valvuloplasty is now being applied to the heart itself. Once positioned, the balloon is inflated to stretch open narrowed mitral and aortic valves—the two valves permitting the bloodflow into and out of, respectively, the left ventricle of the heart.

Effective as it is, however, balloon surgery has limitations. Because the plaque is only pushed back, not removed, about 30 percent of opened coronary arteries close again within 12 months, requiring a repeat operation. Current research is attempting to correct the problem with stents—tiny tubular braces—that are installed to prevent the widened walls from collapsing, but the work remains experimental. More serious are the rare cases where arteries spontaneously collapse shortly after angioplasty; an emergency coronary by-pass team is usually on standby throughout the operation.

SURGERY WITH SOUND

Decidedly more high-tech than angioplasty in its knifeless approach to surgery is the entirely noninvasive technique known as lithotripsy. Using nothing but ultrasound—sound waves of extremely high frequency—lithotripsy succeeds in pulverizing kidney, bladder and gall stones. Most kidney and bladder stones that fail to pass spontaneously in the urine can be treated with medications; others require aggressive intervention. Increasingly, doctors resolve the problem with a completely noninvasive technique called extracorporeal shock wave lithotripsy, or ESWL. First suggested at a social gathering by the physician wife of an aeronautical engineer, ESWL was inspired by the effect of shock waves from aircraft flying at supersonic speeds.

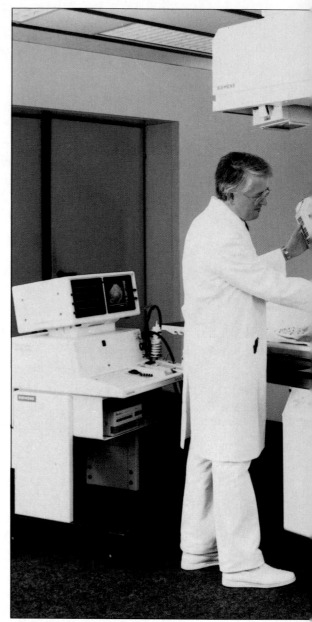

One application of ESWL requires that patients—under either general or regional anesthesia—be precisely positioned in a tub of water. X-ray machines are used to locate and visualize kidney stones in three dimensions, so that they can be lined up with an underwater electrode located at the bottom of the tub. An electrical discharge from the electrode vaporizes some of the tub water, creating a spherical shock wave that passes through the water and the patient's soft tissues; since water and living tissue are similar in acoustic property, almost all the energy created by the shock wave is focused on the brittle matter of the stone, at which it is aimed. About 1,400 shock waves are administered over the span of an hour, turning the stone into fine granules, which pass harmlessly with the urine over a period of days. Because of its resiliency, living bone is relatively unaffected by the shock waves.

Newer ESWL machines transmit shock waves through water contained in a bag placed against the skin. Instead of X rays, ultrasound imaging devices are used to focus the shock waves. Because this technique destroys kidney stones and, more recently, gallstones painlessly—using shock waves of special geometrical shapes, it is commonly practiced as an out-patient procedure without anesthesia.

Like lithotripsy, radiation therapy stands on the cusp of surgery's microcosmic war against disease. While not surgery per se, it shares traits with other "bloodless" techniques. Like lasers, radiotherapy uses electromagnetic radiation to destroy

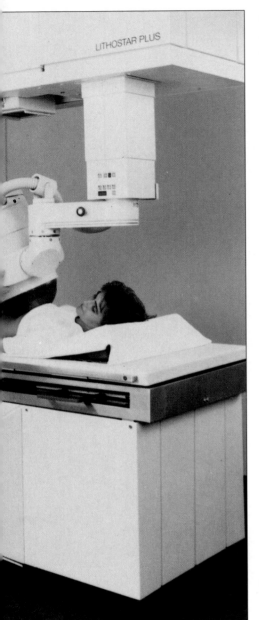

LITHOSTAR PLUS

A patient lies motionless on a table while a doctor, during lithotripsy treatment, uses shock waves emanating from an overhead arm to crush the patient's kidney stones. Composed of mineral salts, the stones are easily located with ultrasound equipment; shock waves are then aimed at the target. Though they pass easily through soft tissues and resilient bone, the waves collide with brittle substances, shattering stones into particles the size of grains of sand.

cells; like lithotripsy, it focuses and delivers energy without knives. The primary application of radiotherapy is to kill cancer, a fight which it often wages in concert with chemotherapy and conventional surgery.

Radiotherapy does its work with high-energy light beams that destroy by colliding with the water molecules making up 70 percent of both normal and cancerous cells. On impact, these ionizing beams cause a transfer, from one molecule to another, of electrons—the tiny particles that orbit around a molecule's nucleus. The resultant structures are no longer electrically balanced, having either one electron too many or one too few, and thus carry either a positive or a negative charge. Called free radicals, their inherent electrical instability allows them to meddle with the cell's genetic material—deoxyribonucleic acid, or DNA—and thus destroy the cell's ability to grow and divide. In some unfortunate cases, free radicals may only injure the cell, causing its DNA structure to mutate; years later, the mutation can manifest itself as a cancer such as leukemia. In short, ionizing radiation can both cure and cause cancer.

To avoid the latter, radiation therapy operates much like a military air strike—hours of preflight planning and mapping get poured into a bombardment that may last only seconds. Computers are employed to superimpose patterns of dose distribution on 3-D images of the patient's body; these images are supplied by CT and MRI scans *(pages 30-33)*. Thus armed, radiation oncologists, or cancer specialists, can calculate the best bombardment angle and the maximum possible dose, subjecting local healthy tissues to the least damage.

Killing tumors with radiation would be an easy job if healthy tissue were not affected in a similar way to cancerous cells. Although normal cells can generally absorb and survive the same radiation dose that will kill cancer cells—in fact, all radiotherapy is based on this principle—their resiliency varies. Consequently, therapy is tricky when a tumor resides in tissue that is hardier than nearby cells. One practice is to implant a radioactive element directly into the tumor; radium or cesium are sometimes used for this purpose. Used for cancers of the head, neck, uterus and prostate, such implants can be temporary or permanent. Some implants, including those for treating mouth cancers, may be installed with a needle while the patient is under local anesthetic. On the other hand, implants for large, deep-seated tumors may require a general anesthetic and an entire surgical team.

Radiation therapy is a long way from basic surgical maneuvers involving knives, needles and thread. Yet, along with techniques such as lithotripsy and laser, it shares the goal of healing through the removal or manipulation of tissue. Cryosurgery and angioplasty, electrosurgery and therapeutic endoscopy also share this tradition, which dates back before the time of Hippocrates. Venerable perhaps, but a time-honored tradition it is not; until the 19th Century, the practice of surgery was regarded as a last resort that often posed more of a threat to well-being than did the problem it purported to cure. The three pillars of aseptic technique, anesthesia and blood transfusion, along with surgery's arsenal of specialized tools, have made possible a multitude of viable treatments for injuries, deformities and countless diseases. Soon, either the term "surgery" will have to be expanded or a new term created to encompass the growing number of sophisticated techniques that, unlike the crude art practiced by barber surgeons of old, not only cut without letting blood, but heal without cutting.

Blueprint for Healing

Ambulance attendants rush into a hospital emergency room with a severely injured accident victim. The emergency staff mobilizes to give the victim priority; after a rapid examination, the attending physicians decide that surgery must be performed as quickly as possible. A coordinator phones ahead to the operating room, and an intern wheels the patient's gurney past staff and other patients and through the labyrinth of corridors to the operating theater. In a situation where seconds count, having to wait for an elevator or travel long, circuitous routes between departments might make all the difference in the world.

Unfortunately, many conventional hospitals do have such problems: Related departments are often far apart; elevators are slow and too few; long hospital corridors are time-consuming, energy-wasting and often confusing to patients and staff alike.

While many hospitals currently are undergoing structural renovation in order to correct some of these problems, new hospitals can avoid them altogether with contemporary designs reflecting a new vision. Wherever possible, architects plan one-story hospitals, precluding the need for elevators; they study traffic flow and group related departments. Even something as mundane as including a crawl space above diagnostic and treatment areas can make a difference; electrical cables and water pipes are easily accessible for repairs, preventing maintenance shut-downs. All wards and departments are allotted extra space to accommodate any new technology that might become available and future hospital expansion is factored into the original blueprint.

This architectural blueprint of the Anna Laberge Hospital in Chateauguay, Quebec, illustrates a modern hospital design. Related hospital services such as emergency, intensive care radiology and surgery are close together. For speed and convenience, a central corridor is used by the general public, while peripheral hallways are reserved for staff and patients.

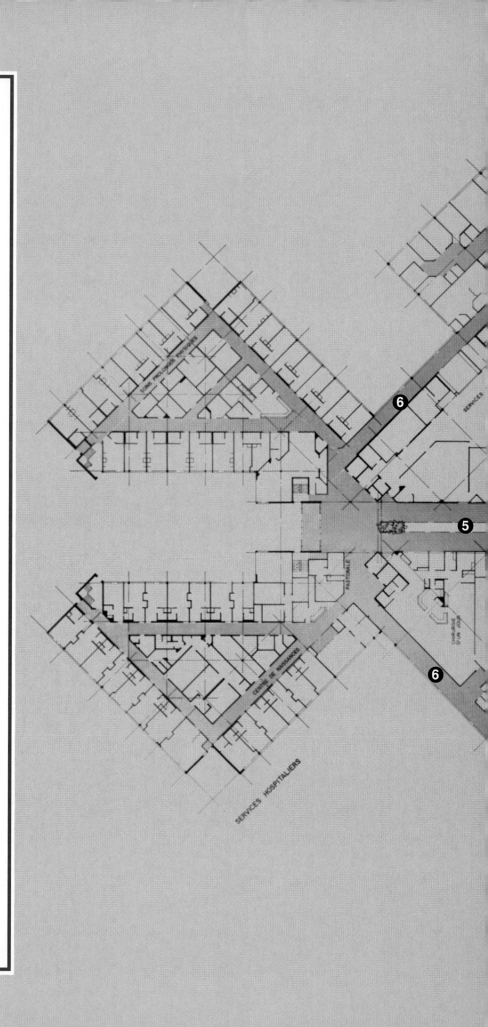

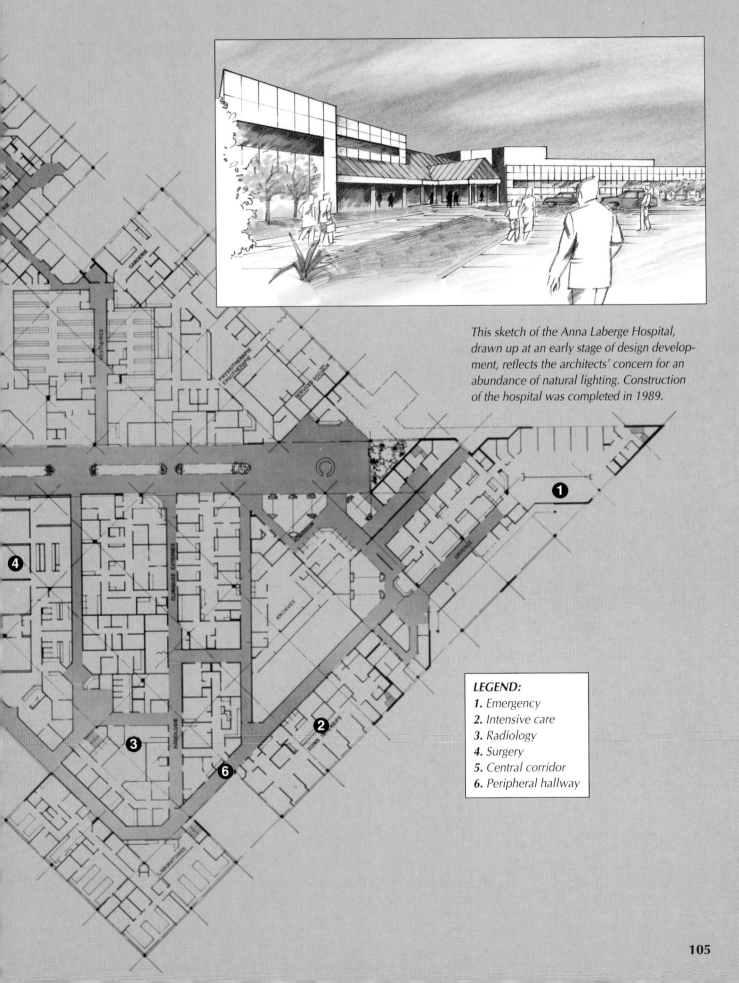

This sketch of the Anna Laberge Hospital, drawn up at an early stage of design development, reflects the architects' concern for an abundance of natural lighting. Construction of the hospital was completed in 1989.

LEGEND:
1. Emergency
2. Intensive care
3. Radiology
4. Surgery
5. Central corridor
6. Peripheral hallway

Hospitality

As well as revolutionizing major structural design, architects and designers are changing the look and feel of hospitals' interior space. The institutional interior ambience associated with many traditional hospitals is often the result of a preponderance of linear hallways, unimaginative colors, the absence of decorative touches and an overwhelming smell of disinfectant solution. Harsh fluorescent lighting all too frequently takes the place of the natural light afforded by windows and skylights. The overall effect of such designs can be a cold and unwelcoming environment that makes patients feel anxious the moment they step through the entrance. It may even retard healing. Studies show that a patient's psychological state has a profound influence on recovery.

Newer hospitals are designed from the outset with patient satisfaction in mind. Architects and interior designers work hard to reproduce a homelike environment for the patient. Pedestrian traffic through the hospital, for example, is often along nonlinear corridors that break up the monotonous view of long, straight hallways; triangular-shaped common areas create more cozy enclosures than rectangular rooms. And the use of soft colors on walls and ceilings brightens hallways and rooms. Windows and skylights admit light and allow patients, staff and visitors to see the ouside world.

Not surprisingly, modern maternity rooms offer the expectant mother a homelike environment. Medical equipment is kept hidden in a cupboard until required. Furnishings such as wallpaper, table lamps and rocking chairs add to this effect. Psychiatric wards incorporate a communal living space, a feature that promotes patient socialization.

Though illness is never pleasant, a comfortable environment promotes recovery.

The mall, or central corridor, of the Anna Laberge Hospital serves as a meeting place for patients, staff and visitors. A skylight, extending the length of the mall, provides natural light and helps to create a warm atmosphere.

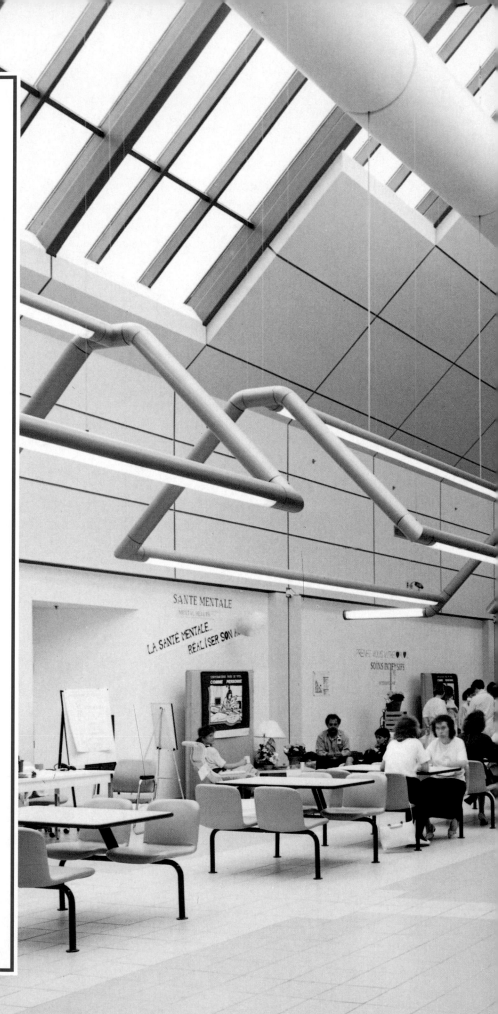

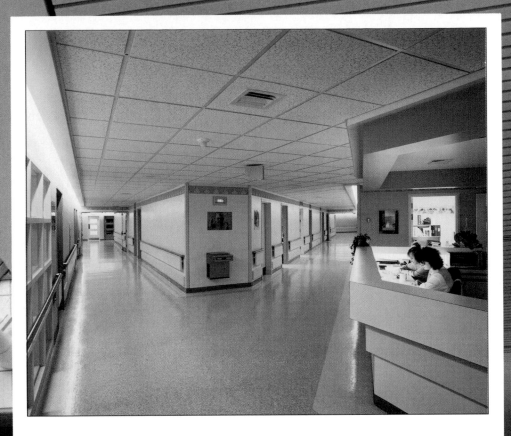

A nurses' station in this maternity ward is strategically positioned, enabling nurses to observe two corridors of patients' rooms simultaneously. The dusty rose and off-white color scheme is soothing for both patients and personnel.

High-Tech Networking

Technology joins forces with architectural design in streamlining the functioning of contemporary hospitals. In the medical laboratory, for instance, automated blood analyzers are able to complete hundreds of tests in a fraction of the time that it previously took technicians to perform the tests manually. Medical imagery such as computerized tomography, used to create X rays of the body in cross sections, has revolutionized diagnosis, permitting physicians to "see" into the body. In the operating theater, new surgical tools, such as lasers, permit surgeons to treat the patient without causing pain or blood loss. And advanced monitoring equipment keeps the surgical team cognizant of every aspect of the patient's physical state during anesthesia.

Perhaps most remarkably, all the medical and administrative information pertaining to a patient, stored in a computer file, can be accessed at consoles located throughout the hospital—even at the patient's bedside. Such accessibility encourages constant communication between hospital departments.

To ensure confidentiality and security, each care-giver uses a password which restricts user access to a select set of data. The staff member with the greatest responsibility, the physician, has access to the entire file, enabling him to call up test results from the medical laboratory or to verify drug administration. Today's hospital reflects a holistic vision of patient care. Rational architectural design and high technology augment the resources available to medicine, resulting in more pleasant health care and the ultimate payoff: a greater number of saved lives.

A computer console next to the patient's bed at Anna Laberge Hospital enables the physician to review the entire patient record while examining the patient. Computer data storage is less prone to loss and error than are conventional paper files.

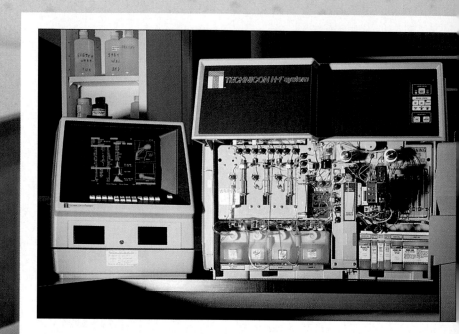

This automated laboratory machine performs blood counts. Test tubes of blood samples, labeled with electronic codes, advance automatically while the machine counts red and white blood cells as well as platelets—blood components necessary for blood clotting. Results appear in tabular and graphic form on a computer screen (left), and may also be printed on paper.

REPLACEMENT PARTS

I n a recent New York City marathon, exhausted runners crossing the finish line were amazed by a fellow competitor who, having completed the race, sat calmly unlacing his shoe—and then went on to unstrap his entire foot and ankle. He had run the grueling 26.2-mile marathon wearing an artificial limb. The Athenian youth who first ran this distance, to report a victory in the battle of the Greeks over the Persians in 490 B.C., was so exhausted by the time he reached Athens that he keeled over dead. That thousands of runners now complete the race every year, pushing their bodies to the limits of endurance is, in itself, cause for wonder. But the fact that some people go the route with limbs, and even organs, that in reality are replacement parts, is a testament both to the human spirit and to medical technology.

The wooden legs of fabled swashbuckling seafarers and the steel-clad forearm of Captain Hook have given way to today's more prosaic—and more useful—electronically controlled legs and arms, artificial hands with movable fingers, polymer knee joints and titanium hips. Thousands of people see the world through corneas either of plastic or of human tissue donated by others. Burn victims grow new skin under a protective coating of grafted tissue that is half organic, half synthetic. Ailing hearts beat time to implanted electronic pacemakers; others fill and empty through valves made of plastic or pig membrane.

Most extraordinary of all, perhaps, are the transplants of live organs. The gift of a heart, kidney or liver is the gift of life itself. It is no wonder that few other advances in medical technology have received such worldwide attention.

The first experimental transplant, on a dog, was performed at the turn of the century in Vienna; physiologist Emerich Ullmann transferred one of the dog's kidneys from its normal position to the animal's neck. The graft succeeded, but a failed attempt to transplant a kidney from one dog to another dog brought the researcher up against a stumbling block that was not immediately understood: Organs trans-

This tennis player demonstrates the freedom, mobility and natural appearance afforded her an her artificial leg. High-tech synthetics and user-conscious design combine to create prostheses—some of which use electrical components—that permit many sports activities.

ferred from one being to another—whether animal or human—invariably incite the recipient's immune system to attack the alien cells. It was not until half a century later, in 1954, that a man, dying of kidney failure, successfully received a kidney from his twin brother at Boston's Peter Bent Brigham Hospital. Genetically identical, the men's immune systems recognized each other's cells as their own. The next big breakthrough was the transplant of a human heart, by Dr. Christiaan Barnard of Capetown, South Africa, in 1967. While this first recipient survived only 18 days, a second heart recipient lived 18 months. Today, some borrowed hearts have been pumping for more than 20 years, a glowing testimony to the progress medical science has made in fighting the rejection process. Similar progress has been made in a number of areas; computerized communications networks and improved organ preservation have increased the number of successful transplants astronomically. These advances have given rise to dramatic medical miracles as life itself is passed from one person to another.

THE GIFT OF LIFE

It is 1 a.m. at a major urban hospital. A 40-year-old man, admitted with severe head injuries after a car accident, has been pronounced brain dead—irreversibly unconscious and unable to breathe, functions that depend on the irreplaceable brainstem, which was destroyed in the accident. The deceased was a lean jogger who ate sensibly, drank socially and did not smoke. He wore glasses at the movies and behind the wheel of his car, but other than that, he had no physical limitations or disabilities. Although he has been pronounced legally dead, the doctors put him on a life-support system to maintain his blood flow. Most of his organs and tissues are still viable—they will be able to function after a short preservation period—and could be transplanted. The medical team checks the optional organ donor form on the back of the victim's driver's license. The man's signature bespeaks his intention to donate.

The instant the accident victim's next of kin has also expressed consent which is mandatory in many jurisdictions, the hospital's transplant coordinator types a list of the donor's organs into a computer network. All transplant centers within the region receive the message. AVAILABLE: liver, pancreas, heart, two lungs, two kidneys and skin.

Immediately, the coordinator's phone rings: A hospital 500 miles away has a potential recipient for a kidney and the pancreas—a 20-year-old diabetic whose pancreas is not producing insulin and who also has kidney failure. In a relatively new procedure, the transplant pancreas can be placed near the kidney while the native pancreas remains in place. The original pancreas will continue to perform a digestive role, while the donor pancreas will produce insulin.

From this point on, time is of the essence. Lost seconds at any stage—from the moment of organ retrieval until the recipient's blood is flowing through the new organ—could result in death. All organs have a built-in time limit. While a preserved kidney can remain viable for up to 48 hours, for instance, the pancreas can only be stored for 24. But before approval of the donor organ for this recipient, doctors must carry out a tissue-typing test to assess the degree of compatibility between donor and potential recipient. Even with the strides made in organ retrieval and transplantation techniques, there remains the grave threat of the body's immune attack on the new organs. To combat deadly microbes—whether fungi, bacteria or viruses—the body's immune system immediately inspects anything foreign and codes it as "other" rather than "self," calling up a formidable army of specialized blood cells. The security code signifying "self" is a substance known as human leukocyte antigen, or HLA, a protein found on the surface of every white blood cell of the body and in all its tissues.

The testing process is fairly complex: Lymphocytes, the white blood cells responsible for immune reaction, are drawn from both the donor and the potential recipient. Each is mixed with a typing reagent—a serum that contains antibodies to certain HLA antigens. Depending on the reactions observed in both the donor's sample and the recipient's, doctors are able to assess the degree of compatibility and the probable strength of the immune response. Identical twins always will have a HLA perfect match—100 percent compatibility. Organs or tissue from other blood relatives will have at least a partial match. But the compatibility of unrelated individuals is a wild card. It could range from 100 percent to none whatsoever.

Once these tests have shown that there is enough compatibility to proceed with the transplant, doctors begin the process of preserving the organ or tissue. An ice-cold solution is perfused, or flushed, through the donor's blood vessels. Because such exquisite timing is involved, the medical community has been working to improve the various perfusion solutions and thereby increase the length of time an organ can remain viable. When the organs are sufficiently cooled—in less than 30 minutes—they are removed from the body and placed in sterile containers on ice. The hospitals keep in constant touch by telephone, so that by the time the donor organs arrive at the recipient's hospital, the patient already has been prepared for the transplant surgery.

A surgical transplant retrieval team hurries an organ cooler from jet to waiting ambulance. After the life support system has been shut off, each organ or tissue has a limited survival period, making transportation of donated organs to potential recipients a critical link in the process.

The operation begins with an incision across the recipient's abdomen. The donor kidney is placed in the left pelvic area, and the kidney's main artery and vein, as well as the ureter—which connects the kidney to the bladder—are stitched to corresponding structures in the recipient. The original kidneys are left in place. The donor pancreas, complete with pancreatic duct—which serves to transport digestive enzymes from the pancreas to the small intestine—is placed on the opposite side of the pelvis. The appropriate blood vessels are attached and the pancreatic duct, still connected to a portion of the donor's small intestine, is stitched to the recipient's bladder.

After the operation, because of the threat of immune rejection, drugs called anti-rejection or immunosuppressants, are administered to tone down the combative response of the body's white blood cells. Though immunosuppressants have made possible successful transplants, they do have definite dis-

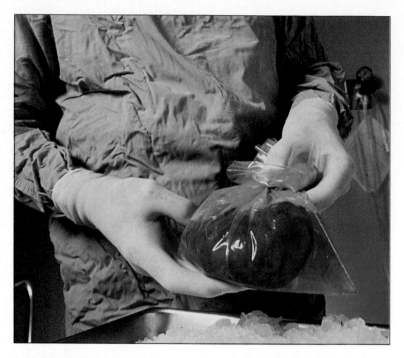

A transplant surgeon lifts a kidney from its ice pack just minutes before surgery is to begin. While temporary freezing delays the cellular decomposition of organs and tissues, it does not prevent it indefinitely. Kidneys cannot be stored for more than two days.

advantages; they have the potential to cause diabetes, early cataracts, a puffy face, excessive hair growth, liver damage, cancer and reduced immunity to infection. For this reason, it is best to administer the drugs in as low doses as possible. And the greater the tissue compatibility between donor and recipient in the first place, the smaller the quantity of drugs the patient will need after transplantation.

Such drugs are usually not necessary in the case of skin allografts—a graft of skin from one person to another—since frequently the transplanted tissue is removed before immune rejection commences. To treat life-threatening burns—at least second-degree burns to roughly 20 percent of the body—donor skin is grafted over damaged tissues, preventing death from loss of fluid and giving the native skin a chance to regenerate. In about two months' time, just before the recipient's body starts to reject the foreign skin, doctors remove the allograft. With less serious burns, surgeons may take some undamaged tissue from the burn victim and graft it to damaged areas. This procedure, called an autograft, succeeds 95 percent of the time because, unlike an allograft, the autograft is recognized as "self" by the patient's immune system.

Because of the continuing threat of rejection and the harsh side effects of immunosuppressive drugs, certain recipients of complex organs such as the heart are virtually chronic patients. They must be monitored continually. For this reason, a transplant such as the heart-lung graft—a transplant of the heart and both lungs—is considered a treatment, rather than a cure.

THE HEART-LUNG GRAFT

By the early 1980s the heart-lung graft was being practiced. Because of the close working relationship between the heart and lungs, the organs are frequently best transplanted as a set. The balancing act between the lungs seems to be very delicate; replacement of only one lung might result in the original lung's robbing the new one of air, while at the same time allowing it to take too much blood.

Surgery begins with a cut through the recipient's sternum, or breastbone, so that the ribcage can be opened. Then the pericardium—a membrane surrounding the heart—is slit open, exposing the heart. The patient is then connected to a heart-lung machine which circulates the blood. Next, the blood vessels that connect the recipient's heart to his body are clamped. The surgeon cuts through the temporarily stopped heart muscle, leaving in place the top portion of the heart where it is connected to the six veins that empty into it. The aorta—a main artery—is cut however, and must be reconnected later.

The donor heart is stitched onto the remaining top portion of the recipient's heart; first the right atrium—upper-right heart chamber—then the left atrium. When the stitching is complete and the heart is placed back into the pericardium, a pacemaker wire is attached to the new heart to shock it into action.

IN THE VANGUARD

While certain organs are only available as the result of death—heart, pancreas, a complete set of lungs—individual kidneys can be successfully donated by a family member, since a normal existence is possible with one. Transplantation between family members can take place without a long wait for a donor organ, and often has the advantage of greater compatibility. Now, scientists are refining a type of intrafamilial transplant to treat fatal liver disease. Unlike kidneys, livers do not come in pairs, but recent experiments have taken a small portion of a parent's liver and given it to dying offspring. The child's liver is removed and the new portion is stitched in its place; over time, it grows to a normal size. Meanwhile, the parent is able to function normally with a liver about two-thirds of its original size.

Within a decade, the medical community is expected to have perfected transplant operations that are little more than experiments today. Cells from the adrenal glands of fetuses, for example, are being experimentally transplanted into the brains of adults with Parkinson's disease where it is hoped they will produce dopamine, the substance that these patients are missing. Results have shown some lessening of physical symptoms—tremor, rigidity and difficulty initiating movement. And, in the case of a family that carried the genetic blood disease known as Fanconi's anemia, blood was taken from the umbilical cord of the family's healthy newborn girl and transplanted into the bone marrow of her older brother who had the family disease. The girl's blood cells multiplied into a new blood-cell population and completely cured her brother of his otherwise fatal ailment.

As well, scientists expect to extend the period of organ storage. Kidneys, livers, hearts and lungs cannot be preserved in a bank the way corneas, bone and blood now are because these organs cannot tolerate the lack of blood for a long period of time. Recent experiments use a chemical "hibernation induction trigger" extracted from the blood of hibernating woodchucks. When injected with the substance, the survival time of the canine organs increased from 16.2 to 43.4 hours and they functioned well after transplantation. Scientists hope that measures such as these, when they are able to be tested on humans, will save lives, particularly in situations where donor organs must travel great distances before being transplanted.

To prevent the tragedy of having people die while waiting for a donor organ to become available, doctors are teaming up with a host of other professionals to create viable facsimiles of organs, tissues and cells. Complex biomedical teams

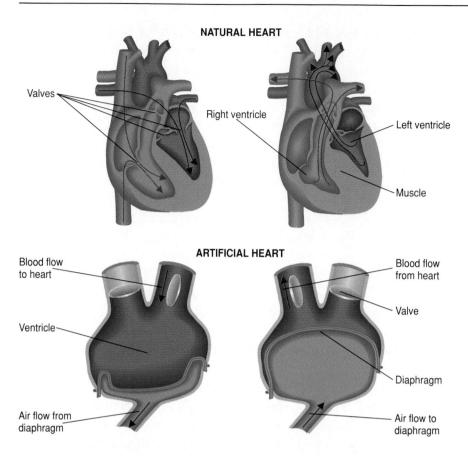

NATURAL HEART

Valves

Right ventricle

Left ventricle

Muscle

ARTIFICIAL HEART

Blood flow to heart

Blood flow from heart

Valve

Ventricle

Diaphragm

Air flow from diaphragm

Air flow to diaphragm

ARTIFICIAL HEART

The illustrations at left show how a natural heart and an artifical heart return oxygen-spent blood to the lungs and pump oxygenated blood to the body. The human heart contains four blood chambers—two atria and two ventricles—surrounded by muscle. Blood flows from the atria to the ventricles, filling them. When the ventricles are full, the muscle contracts and forces blood out of the ventricles. Valves control the direction of blood flow, indicated by the arrows on the diagrams. Blood in the right side of the heart is sent to the lungs for oxygenation; freshly oxygenated blood in the left side is pumped into a main artery, which distributes blood to the body. An artificial heart, although implanted in the body, must remain connected to an external power source and a supply of compressed air. As ventricles fill with blood, a diaphragm is forced to the base of the ventricle. Once the ventricles are filled to capacity, air flows into the diaphragms, inflating them and forcing the blood to flow out of the ventricles, directed by valves.

consist of biochemists, biologists, immunologists, hematologists, pathologists, surgeons, veterinarians and engineers.

Working together, the team carefully analyzes the mechanisms of tissue or an organ—the heart, say—and designs a device to duplicate its function. After a design plan has been agreed upon, a prototype is manufactured and tested over the course of many years. First trials often involve a mechanical simulation—a hydraulic replication of circulation to test an artificial heart, for example—then the device is implanted in a laboratory animal. Months of study, showing promising results, are required prior to government approval to carry out clinical trials on humans; if these succeed, the device can be marketed.

Of primary concern is that the artificial organ or tissue be biodurable, that is strong and durable enough to do its work in the biological environment. It must also be biocompatible, not causing damage to the animal's own tissues and not eliciting an immune reaction. An initial step in this area was the discovery, in 1938, that glass implants were both biocompatible and biodurable. Now, with the aid of computers, bioengineers can custom create materials from glass, ceramics, metal alloys and plastics. Molecule by molecule, they can design synthetics according to doctors' specifications.

Scientists hold great hope for a new category of materials described as biosynthetic—a marriage of natural and synthetic materials. Biosynthetic skin, for example, shows great promise in the treatment of burn patients. American chemist I.V. Yannas and his surgeon partner J.F. Burke have synthesized a temporary skin—not yet commercially available—consisting of a natural and a synthetic layer. The bottom sheet—replacing the fibrous inner skin layer, called the dermis—mimics the chemical composition and the complex fibrous weave of the scaffolding in which the body's cells are embedded to form skin tissue. This layer uses natural materials: shark cartilage and cowhide collagen—an insoluble fibrous protein that gives tissue its connective properties. The top sheet, equivalent to the outer skin layer, called the epidermis, is made of a synthetic silicone-rubber blend. Two weeks after the biosynthetic skin is grafted over the burn, doctors remove the protective synthetic layer and graft a piece of the patient's own epidermis in its place; at this point, the body's natural enzymes have broken down the scaffold of natural tissue, leaving a rebuilt dermis beneath the grafted epidermis.

WONDERS OF BIOENGINEERING

Great strides also have been made in developing artificial organs constructed of materials that, while not biosynthetic, are nonetheless biocompatible. But the material is only one of many important factors involved. The evolution of circulatory system prostheses, artificial hearts or valves, for example, is a perfect study of the multiple concerns facing designers of any replacement part.

One of the most exciting creations in the bioengineering field was the first artificial heart. The task was a complex one, for the heart is a complex organ. In its function of circulating oxygen and nutrients to the body's cells, the heart pumps five quarts of blood per minute. It also works without cease; the average heart beats more than 2.5 billion times in the course of a lifetime and knows when to speed up and when to slow down. Any artificial copy of this dedicated machine would have to be supremely engineered.

Among the first artificial versions of the human heart, the Jarvik-7 was researched and developed for 20 years before being implanted in a cardiac patient in 1982. Unlike a real human heart, which pumps by contracting and expanding, this mechanical version, named after its inventor, Dr. Robert Jarvik, pumps blood by pneumatic pressure from an outside source of compressed air. The air moves via tubes inserted into the patient. Besides valve breakdowns and the six-foot-long cords connecting the patient's chest to an external power source, one of the major problems with the

HEART-LUNG MACHINE

Temporarily circumventing the heart and lungs during open-heart surgery, blood is circulated and oxygenated by heart-lung bypass equipment (below), which takes over the roles of the heart and lungs. Tubes, inserted in the heart's two main veins, transport blood from the body to the machine and return oxygenated blood into a large artery.

1

BLOOD FROM
PATIENT

2

4

BLOOD TO
PATIENT

3

1. Blood reservoir. The blood from the patient enters the reservoir and is sent through a series of filters that remove any bubbles and debris. The reservoir stores an extra supply of blood taken from the patient for use during the surgery.

2. Pump. The blood is sent via tubing through a pump that provides the force to circulate the blood to an oxygenator and to the patient. Other pumps, connected directly to the patient, send a chilled sterile solution to cool the patient's chest; another pump provides suction to draw waste material from the chest cavity.

3. Heat Exchanger. As the blood passes through the heat exchanger, it is cooled during surgery and rewarmed following the operation.

4. Oxygenator. The oxygenator infuses the blood with oxygen. Tubing, connected to the oxygenator, delivers the oxygenated blood to the patient's circulatory system.

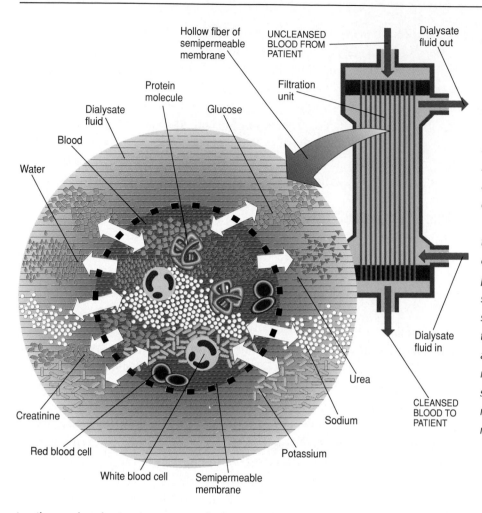

Hollow fiber of semipermeable membrane

UNCLEANSED BLOOD FROM PATIENT

Dialysate fluid out

Protein molecule

Filtration unit

Glucose

Dialysate fluid

Blood

Water

Dialysate fluid in

Urea

CLEANSED BLOOD TO PATIENT

Creatinine

Sodium

Red blood cell

Potassium

White blood cell

Semipermeable membrane

ARTIFICIAL KIDNEY

Individuals with faulty kidneys must have their blood cleansed regularly in the filtration unit of an artificial kidney, or dialysis machine, illustrated here. Drawn from the patient's arm by catheter, uncleansed blood is filtered through the machine's semipermeable membrane; suction and a plasma-like cleansing solution, called dialysate fluid, are used to remove wastes. Water, creatinine and urea diffuse through the membrane, while red and white blood cells and protein molecules—too large to pass through it—remain. Desirable substances such as glucose, potassium and sodium are free to come and go through the membrane, with the result that equal amounts settle on either side; in order to maintain an appropriate balance of these substances. As uncleansed blood is removed, purified blood is continually returned to the patient's body.

Jarvik was that the implant was not biocompatible. Its lining obstructed the smooth flow of blood by snagging blood platelets and fibrin which stuck together and sometimes turned into dangerous clots. As a result of these and other complications, the Jarvik heart is now used in the United States only as a bridge to transplantation, while the patient awaits a suitable donor heart.

Problems with the Jarvik, and other artificial organs, inspired methods of improving blood flow thus reducing the potential for blood clots. Through a process called biolization, for example, the polymer interior of an artificial heart is chemically coated, sometimes incorporating ingredients from the user's own blood. By smoothing blood flow, this technique reduces the likelihood of blood clot formation and blood cell destruction.

As technology advances to reduce the biochemical complications of exposing blood to synthetic materials, researchers grow more audacious in their push to devise a more efficient mechanical heart. One research program, at the Cleveland Clinic Foundation, has produced a biocompatible and permanently implantable heart. The total artificial heart—TAH—is powered by an internal battery pack implanted along the ribcage. For most of the day the patient wears an external belt-pack battery, which provides the electric current that passes through the skin and recharges the pack to drive the heart's motor. The battery belt can be removed for up to 40 minutes at a time, allowing the user a relatively unrestricted life. An even freer lifestyle could be achieved by 1994, when researchers at the Foundation

INSULIN PUMP

A boon to diabetics—who may require three insulin shots per day—the insulin pump is permanently implanted in the abdomen or the chest wall. The average titanium pump weighs less than 6 ounces and measures 3.4 inches in diameter. It contains up to a 21-day supply of insulin and can be refilled with a hypodermic needle. The reservoir is surrounded by a fluorocarbon propellant (blue) that expands when heated by body temperture, forcing insulin to flow out of the reservoir through a catheter that is connected to a blood vessel, thus providing the diabetic with a continuous, steady infusion.

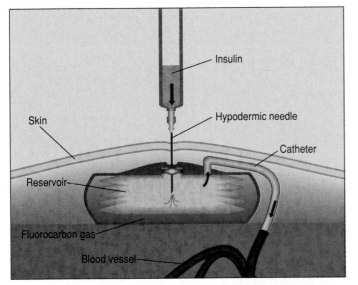

hope to have completed the development of a thermal pump that will function up to eight hours between recharges.

Even when a natural human heart is repaired surgically, artificial organ machinery occasionally plays a role. So traumatic are some open-heart operations that the surgeon may not be able to start up the heart again after repairing it; this has led to the development of a tiny turbine-in-a-tube called the Hemopump. Inserted into the patient's groin, it is threaded up through the blood vessels into the heart and is connected to an outside motor by thin wire cables. The pump assumes most of the heart's workload, giving it a few days to recover. Doctors are somewhat surprised that the pump works, and now have to re-examine their long-held belief that the circulatory system would not tolerate a continuous, non-pulsing blood flow, which is what the motorized turbo-blade provides.

Rather than an entirely new heart, many cardiac patients need only a new heart valve. Most valves are made of metals, polymers and ceramics and are extremely biodurable, designed to last the normal life of the patient.

Slightly more than half of all implanted valves are completely synthetic; the rest are biosynthetic. Aortic valves—frequently taken from pigs—are outfitted with a metal or plastic support to facilitate implantation. These biosynthetic valves are less durable than synthetic, mechanical valves, although some may function well for more than 10 years. They usually deteriorate gradually enough to permit elective replacement surgery.

Meanwhile, scientists continue to search for the perfect artificial blood vessel. For the last 30 years, researchers have been developing the potential of two biocompatible polymers known for their stability, strength, suturability and smooth-flow surface: Dacron and Teflon—the latter also used in non-stick cookware. Both polymers are widely used as artificial blood vessels, especially to bypass cranial and coronary arteries. Although they are the best materials used for artificial blood vessels to date, they nevertheless can result in some blood clot formation and infection. Researchers currently are working on finding solutions to these frustrating problems.

Incompatibility between artificial organs and the human body is a problem that scientists have grappled with in their efforts to refine the heart-lung machine. In use since 1953, the heart-lung machine is a complex system of tubes and pumps that takes over the duties of circulating and oxygenating blood while open-heart surgery is being performed.

Early heart-lung machines damaged red blood cells—causing the cell membranes to rupture and spill their contents—resulting in severe complications. Improved fluid mechanics to reduce shear stress on the blood cells and better biocompatible materials lining the heart-lung machine have permitted heart-lung bypass to become a routine procedure in cardiac surgery.

Diseased lungs can be assisted by means of a new, more biocompatible, temporary artificial lung, the intravascular oxygenator—IVOX. Unlike old-style temporary artificial lungs—which function outside the body and therefore require a

The Ultimate Transplant

In a ground-breaking procedure in September 1990, doctors injected more than a billion genetically altered cells into the bloodstream of a gravely ill girl to whom any cold or ear infection might prove fatal. The child was suffering from ADA deficiency, a genetic disease that debilitates the immune system. And her hope lay in this first approved clinical use of gene therapy.

Each of the human body's billions of cells is composed of chromosomes; each chromosome is composed of thousands of genes; and each gene is a small segment of DNA, or deoxyribonucleic acid. Many genes contain instructions for the manufacture of particular proteins that are vital for body function. Defective or missing genes can result in genetic diseases such as hemophilia, muscular dystrophy and immune system disorders.

Gene therapy may provide medicine with a technique for correcting genetic mistakes. In the 1970s, scientists discovered that segments of the DNA molecule can be replaced with a segment from a healthy cell.

Altering a person's genes is not without risk, however. If a gene is accidentally attached to the wrong segment of a chromosome it may hinder another gene from producing a protein or cause it to manufacture too little or too much. And gene therapy raises ethical concerns. These techniques could be used to alter the genetic makeup of sperm, eggs and young embryo, not only to circumvent an inherited disease, but possibly to "improve" on nature.

Despite these concerns, this revolutionary new procedure is advancing. It already has produced promising results in its first patient—the girl suffering from ADA deficiency—and has opened the door to a whole new realm of possible cures that treat illness by correcting the genetic cause.

These illustrations show the five major stages of gene therapy—an experimental cure for inherited disorders.

2. The Vehicle
This cross section of a virus—rendered harmless by genetic engineering—shows the gene spliced into the virus's genetic material. Viruses are used to transport the desired gene to a sample of the patient's cells.

1. The Instructions
Gene therapy begins in the lab when a segment of a chromosome, or gene—containing the instructions for the manufacture of a missing protein—is isolated, and cut out of a healthy donor cell. The chromosome is made of deoxyribonucleic acid (DNA), which is shaped like a twisted rope ladder *(above)*.

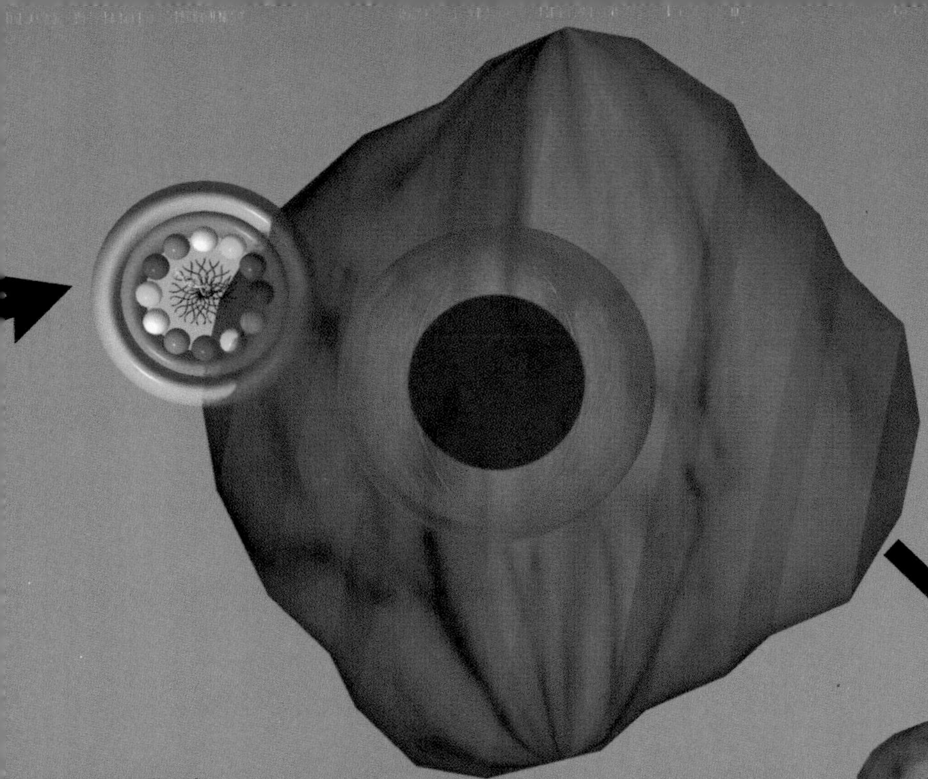

3. The Infiltration
The virus is allowed to infect a sample of the patient's abnormal stem cells—precursors of blood cells—carrying with it the desired gene. The virus's genetic material integrates with the cell's genetic material in its nucleus, illustrated above as a black circle.

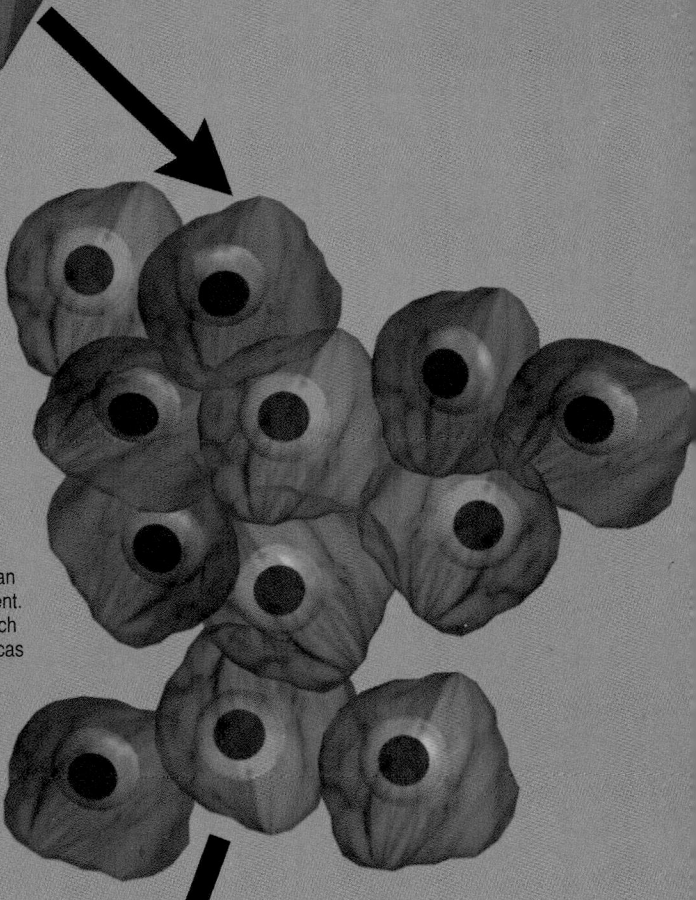

4. The Supply
The genetically altered cells reproduce in an incubator until a sufficient quantity is present. The cells spontaneously multiply under such ideal conditions, producing billions of replicas containing the desired gene.

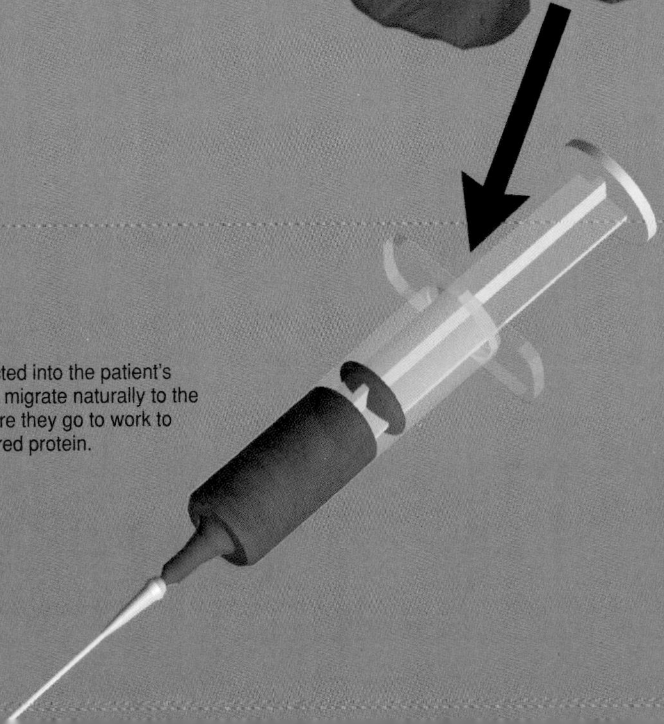

5. The Delivery
The cells are injected into the patient's bloodstream; they migrate naturally to the bone marrow where they go to work to produce the required protein.

121

blood-pumping system and blood-thinning drugs—the IVOX is positioned in the blood vessel leading back to the heart. By carrying out exchanges of the blood's gases within the body itself, it minimizes the likelihood of potentially lethal blood clots. The device uses a bundle of minuscule plastic tubes that are dotted with pores and coated with a gas-permeable membrane containing an anticoagulant. When threaded into the principal vein in the abdomen and chest—the vena cava—the long thin tubes allow the exchange of gases in the blood before it even reaches the lungs. A vacuum pump outside the body pulls oxygen into the IVOX device, also withdrawing the blood's carbon dioxide through the IVOX tubes.

KIDNEYS AND PANCREASES

Improved biocompatibility has benefited not only patients with failing hearts and lungs, but also the world's estimated 300,000 patients on dialysis—blood purification to compensate for failing kidneys. Like all the body's organs, the kidneys are composed of millions of cells that work together to accomplish a job; the job of the kidneys is to purify the blood of all metabolic wastes, which they do continuously, cleansing an average of 47.5 gallons of blood each day. But when the kidneys cannot keep up the pace, the blood must be purified artificially; three times a week, chronic kidney patients are hooked up to a special washing device called a hemodialysis machine, or dialyzer. A selective membrane in the dialyzer, aided by suction and a cleaning fluid called dialysate, allows metabolic wastes to diffuse out of the blood.

Of course, artificial kidney machines do not function 24 hours a day, every day, the way real kidneys do. And patients must travel to a hospital and spend a certain number of hours each week attached to the machine. A liberating alternative is a technique called continuous ambulatory peritoneal dialysis—CAPD. This method allows the person to carry out the process at home, rather than having to go to the hospital several times a week. Unlike hemodialysis, CAPD exchanges new blood for old within the body itself, even while the patient is walking around. The patient has a catheter surgically implanted into the abdominal, or peritoneal, cavity. Connected to the catheter is a plastic bag of dialysate fluid, which flows into the peritoneal cavity by gravity when the patient raises the bag to shoulder level—the patient is free to tuck the bag under his clothing while going about his daily activities. The dialysate fluid flows throughout the abdominal cavity, pulling wastes and excess water from the blood in the capillaries near the surface of the peritoneal membrane.

This membrane, which lines the peritoneal cavity, consists of a single layer of cells overlying tissue that is rich with blood capillaries. The walls of these tiny blood vessels are permeable to many chemical substances, since nutrients must be able to leave the blood to enter the body's cells. The peritoneal membrane acts as a filter, permitting waste products and excess water to pass through. These substances enter the dialysate fluid. When all the blood's wastes have been absorbed, the patient unrolls the empty plastic bag, which is still hooked to the abdominal catheter, and lowers it below the level of the abdomen. Gravity causes the toxin-laden fluid to drain into the bag, which is then discarded.

While artificial kidneys take a natural substance—blood—and submit it to a chemical transformation, machines designed to replace the pancreas work essen-

Artificial Cells

At the microscopic level of artificial organ research, Dr. Thomas Chang of McGill University in Montreal has developed replacements for the smallest possible body unit: the cell.

One type is designed to purify the blood when the kidneys cannot do the job. Stored in a two-by-five-inch tube that is connected to the circulating blood for two hours per session, the microscopic cells have a polymer skin; this semipermeable membrane allows wastes to enter the cell, while preventing the contents from spilling out.

When wastes enter the artificial cell, they are adsorbed by charcoal granules within. Used in the treatment of kidney failure, the charcoal adsorbs certain wastes but not others; however, when used in tandem with standard dialysis, it shortens treatment time by up to one half.

Another project of Chang's is artificial blood cells; these cells contain natural hemoglobin—the oxygen-carrying compo-nent of red blood cells—enveloped in artificial membranes along with special enzymes. Blood can be taken from natural red blood cells and repackaged. The hemoglobin can be enveloped in one of a number of possible membranes, including polymers, proteins and fat-soluble materials known as lipids.

A prime advantage of repackaging hemoglobin is that, while the external membranes of natural red blood cells are marked with chemical labels indicating blood type A, B, AB or O artificial cells can be accepted by anyone. Also, it is possible to sterilize the artificial cells, ensuring freedom from contamination with diseases such as hepatitis or acquired immunodeficiency syndrome (AIDS).

Meanwhile, experiments are being carried out with other kinds of artificial cells, containing medications, enzymes, absorbents or cell cultures. These cells are used in liver support, diabetes and enzyme therapy.

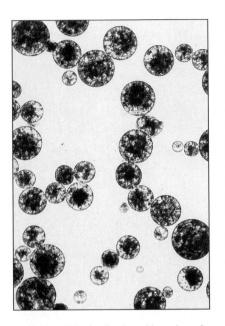

Artificial red blood cells, viewed here through an optical microscope, contain hemoglobin extracted from natural cells. Some artificial blood cells may be as small as four hemoglobin molecules.

tially as delivery pumps. Their job is to supply the hormone insulin. The healthy pancreas regulates how the body converts food to fuel—the sugar known as glucose—and how it stores and uses this fuel. Insulin facilitates the storage of glucose in the liver and muscles for future energy needs and promotes the synthesis of proteins for muscle-building. It also decreases the production of toxic substances and removes harmful fatty acids from the blood.

Diabetics, whose pancreas does not produce an adequate supply of insulin, do not receive the full benefit of the food they eat. Although a strict diet is essential, the diabetic may become seriously ill, even die, without an artificial insulin-regulating mechanism. As an alternative to painful insulin injections, the first insulin pump was implanted successfully in a diabetic in 1980. Installed in the chest, the device consists of a reservoir of insulin that is released at a steady rate; not only does it avoid the physical pain of regular injections, it also prevents excessive highs and lows of dosage. In 1986, a new innovation upgraded the insulin pump into a computer-controlled, battery-powered intelligent organ. The programmable implantable medication system permits diabetics to administer precise doses of insulin. After being implanted, a prescribed dose of insulin, based on the patient's individual needs, is programmed into the system. Although the amount of the regular infusions are preset, the patient can override the programmed dose with a pocket programmer if necessary, to compensate for variations in normal activity—jogging, for example, might necessitate a temporary alteration of dosage.

Although this system simplifies insulin administration, it has room for improvement; unlike the real pancreas, the device does not monitor the patient's blood sugar. That is the next step. A small glucose sensor is being developed which could accurately monitor blood glucose levels and be implanted under the diabetic's skin, delivering insulin in much the same way as the healthy pancreas does, while leaving the diabetic free from worry about his daily dosages.

Still in the experimental stage is a device that would use the natural pancreatic cells that actually produce insulin. Recently a surgeon in Texas invented a bio-compatible plastic tube containing a chamber filled with cells that can be inserted—catheter-like—into a vein, where the cells are nourished by blood and continue to produce insulin. So far, the invention has only been tested on animals.

From external machines constructed of totally synthetic materials to implantable devices incorporating natural cells, the field of artificial organs is vast and varied. Yet, some researchers have gone a step further and are producing substitute cells and tissues. Most effort in this area has focused on cell packages with artificial membranes that mimic material from natural kidney, pancreas and red blood cells. However, one of the most promising substitutes for blood is a liquid substance made up entirely of non cellular molecules, called perfluorocarbons, PFCs. Introduced to the scientific world by Dr. Leland Clark, of the University of Cincinnati College of Medicine in Ohio, PFCs are capable of carrying oxygen like red blood cells. Rodents, when immersed in a beaker of PFCs, proved to be able to breathe the liquid. While trials have used PFCs in transfusions, they do have certain unresolved problems. They tend to block circulation and do not deliver oxygen as efficiently as red blood cells; on the other hand, because they have never been in the body of another individual, they are disease-free, compatible with all blood types and non allergenic. Scientists are optimistic that PFCs may lead medicine to a viable form of artificial blood.

THE BIONIC BODY

Anyone who has ever received an electric shock knows that the body is an excellent conductor. Each of the body's 100 million million cells is a two-way transmitter, whose daily work involves continuously receiving and sending electrical signals. Today, the conductivity of the body is being exploited by a new generation of body parts. From electrophysical stimulators to electromechanical prostheses and electronic implants, the latest wave in biomedical engineering has vastly improved, even saved, countless lives. The beneficiaries are the world's first truly bionic men and women.

One of the most exciting advances is the use of electricity to stimulate the body's nerves—the body's version of electrical wires—in order to modify sensory perception, including pain, as well as to trigger muscular action. A battery-powered electrical source, which may or may not be implanted within the body, sends electricity to implanted electrodes that are either very close to, or in direct contact with, the nerve in question.

A pain remedy known as spinal cord stimulation—SCS—has been the focus of intense research for the last 20 years. The spinal cord is connected to the brain and descends the length of the backbone. Connected to the body's major nerves, it is essential to most neural functions. If the cord is damaged or destroyed, so are the underlying nerves; if the cord is stimulated in a certain spot, so are the nerves

THE BODY SHOP

Through the marvels of modern technology, medicine is able to create devices that replace or enhance normal human structures or functions. With each passing year, the field of bioengineering introduces more prostheses and implants, while refining still others. Advances in all areas of science permit the merging of new concepts, leading ultimately to replacement parts that are more durable, more efficient and more adaptable to the human body.

One of the greatest challenges to any artificial body part is the biochemical environment of the body itself. The immune system attacks most synthetic materials, and few can withstand the long-term effects of the humid, saline climate in the body. Substances that can exist well in this environment are termed biocompatible.

Titanium, for example, has revolutionized structural implants, especially joints such as hips. Small joints can be reconstructed, complete with flexible hinges, using a pliable synthetic called silicone elastomer; the same material is used in the cosmetic recontouring of body parts such as the breast, nose and penis.

While many artificial parts are of structural or esthetic importance, others—such as the artificial heart—are designed to function on their own to replace a faulty body mechanism. New myoelectric limbs lend mobility to amputees, cooperating with remnant muscles that activate electric signals to move the arm or leg. Still other replacements interact directly with the body's nervous system. In the ear, for example, electronic devices called cochlear implants are gathering soundwaves, encoding them as electrical signals and sending them directly to the brain.

Multifocal intraocular lens prostheses
Restore near and distant sight following cataract removal.

Cochlear implant
Converts soundwaves to electrical signals and uses them to stimulate auditory nerve in cases of deafness.

Heart pacemaker implant
Electrically stimulates heart contractions in cases of abnormal rhythm.

Breast and nipple prostheses
Provide support for cosmetic enlargement or rebuilding following surgical removal due to disease.

Pectus implant
Expands chest in patients born with depressed breastbone.

Electric arm prosthesis
Replaces limb following trauma or surgical removal due to disease.

Spinal fixation device
Stabilizes vertebrae after fracture or tumor removal.

Hip ball prosthesis
Replaces socket joint following disease or trauma.

Blood vessel prosthesis
Replaces arteries damaged by atherosclerosis.

Adjustable femoral and knee hinge prosthesis
Replaces knee joint and femur bone removed from growing children due to cancer.

Ligament prosthesis
Replaces damaged ligament in knee.

Ankle prosthesis
Replaces talus bone and part of tibia bone following disease or trauma.

Great toe hinge prosthesis
Replaces joint following bunion removal.

Orbital floor implants
Provide support to eyeballs following bone removal due to disease.

Ear and nose prostheses
Provide support for cosmetic recontouring.

Jaw prosthesis
Provides support for jaw reconstruction following bone loss due to disease or trauma.

Shoulder ball prosthesis
Replaces socket joint following damage due to disease or trauma.

Artificial heart implant
Temporarily circulates blood while patient awaits heart transplant.

Elbow hinge prosthesis
Replaces joint following damage due to disease or trauma.

Finger hinge prostheses
Replace joints following damage due to disease or trauma.

Tendon implant
Provides temporary tube through which permanent tendon graft is threaded during surgical reconstruction following disease or trauma.

Penile prosthesis
Provides support for reconstruction following trauma.

Testicular implant
Provides form when missing at birth, following surgical removal due to disease or after trauma.

Flexible leg and foot prosthesis
Replaces limb following trauma or surgical removal due to disease.

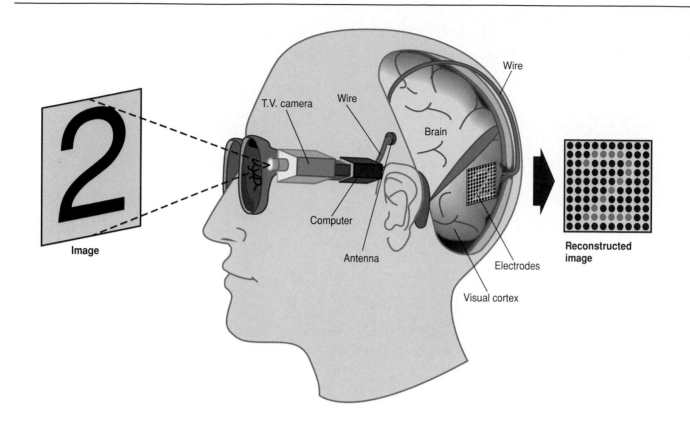

Image

Reconstructed image

Wire

T.V. camera

Wire

Brain

Computer

Antenna

Electrodes

Visual cortex

in that same area, influencing the bodily functions they control. This knowledge is proving instrumental in the treatment of chronic pain. Interestingly, nerves cannot carry two sensations—such as pleasure and pain—at the same moment; by stimulating the spinal cord to block electrochemical signals that mediate sensation, doctors can often scramble signals of discomfort from the lower back or, in the case of the fabled "phantom limb," from nerves that formerly made contact with a once-painful member that has since been amputated. SCS, using an external or an implantable power source and implanted electrodes close to the spinal cord, provides pain relief for about half the designated patients. Because the treatment is not universally successful, doctors often treat the patient first with a stimulating system that uses electrodes placed on the surface of the skin—rather than implanted electrodes—in order to estimate the potential effectiveness of SCS before going ahead with the surgery.

With the external stimulating system, called transcutaneous electrical nerve stimulation, TENS, electricity must first pass through the skin before reaching local nerves. Used for both acute and chronic pain, it frequently relieves pain associated with childbirth, muscle spasms, athletic injury and arthritis. Still, although a simple and straightforward system for relieving localized pain, TENS is not as effective as the direct nerve stimulation of SCS in the reduction of severe, chronic pain, or pain that covers a large area of the body.

As well as mediating pain, electrical nerve stimulation is making exciting headway in problems involving other senses. Many blind individuals still have some undamaged eye tissue. Capitalizing on this knowledge and making use of intact ocular tissue, researchers in Canada and the United States are trying to help the blind see with an electronic eye.

ARTIFICIAL EYE

In most cases of blindness, the eyes are at fault while the brain and related nerves are healthy; the artificial eye circumvents the problem by sending visual data, in the form of electronic messages, directly to the brain region responsible for sight. While early experiments used visual images created with a computer, other tests have utilized a small television camera; already in existence, a matchbox-size TV camera—such as the one illustrated—may soon be mounted on glasses or installed in eye sockets. The image is then processed by a mini-computer and sent as a radio signal to an antenna within the skull, and ultimately to silicon electrodes implanted in the brain. The electrodes give minute electrical shocks to nerve cells in the brain region known as the visual cortex—a processing point in the physiological journey of all visual data. With each shock, the subject sees a dot of light; a conglomeration of dots produces an actual visual image with a definable form, reminiscent of a dot matrix printout.

Every visual image begins as light that is transformed into an encoded electrochemical message by the retina—the light-sensitive membrane at the back of the eye. Then it is sent via the optic nerve to the brain. By electrically stimulating cells in a region of the brain called the visual cortex, it is possible to circumvent the eye entirely, triggering a light show in the person's head. Still in the experimental stage, brain-implantable electronic eyes send computer-programmed patterns of electric signals to select neurons, producing dots of light; by manipulating the dots' pattern, it is possible to create rudimentary images, similar to those forming the letters used in braille.

For those with partial sight, so-called television glasses are being developed. The glasses use two small imaging lenses, which transmit a picture of the immediate environment by way of optical fibers to a battery-powered portable computer. The computer then converts the light images into electronic signals, which are finally reconverted to light images—superior to the viewer's partial sight—and displayed on minute TV screens on the lenses' inside surfaces.

Profoundly deaf people, like the blind, may have external sensory tissues that are damaged, while operative nerves remain intact. Because of the cooperative roles of ear and brain, electronic devices known as cochlear implants can now stimulate the intact nerves, leading ultimately to the production of sound.

Cochlear implants transform soundwaves into an encoded electrical current, then spirit this current past the damaged parts of the ear to the functioning nerves; the nerves further transform the electrical current into an electrochemical one—utilizing both electrical and chemical energy—and carry the message to decoding centers in the brain. Provided the deaf person still has some functioning neurons in the ear, a cochlear implant may allow him to hear for the first time in years.

MAKING MUSCLES WORK

As well as facilitating sensory experience, electrical stimulation can also trigger muscular activity. Possibly the most far-reaching application of muscular stimulation is the heart pacemaker, used by patients whose heartbeat is too slow or erratic to meet their circulatory requirements, particularly during periods of physical exertion. When it first appeared, in the 1950s, the pacemaker was a cumbersome external device. The earliest model, called the Zoll, delivered 100-volt pulses to the patient's heart via electrodes protuding from the chest. Although the Zoll saved many lives by stimulating the heart muscle to contract, its high-energy pulses hurt and burned the skin so badly that some patients suicidally ripped off the lifegiving electrodes rather than endure the pain.

Toward the end of the 1950s, Zoll's bulky shock-maker gave way to a gentler pacemaker. Designed by an unlikely duo—a doctor and a TV repairman—the prototype was assembled in just a month and, by 1957, was ready to be adapted for

COCHLEAR IMPLANT

Deafness caused within the ear's external machinery can frequently be ameliorated with a cochlear implant, if nerves leading to the brain are still intact—and usually they are. Sounds detected by an external microphone are converted to electrical signals by a speech processor, then transmitted as radio waves to a receiver surgically installed beneath the skin. From the receiver, the electrical signals are conveyed to electrodes implanted in the inner ear—or cochlea—then on to the auditory nerve. Finally, the signals are delivered to the brain, which decodes these electrical signals as sounds.

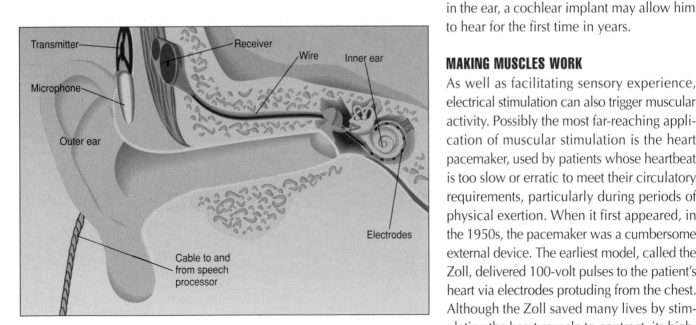

Transmitter
Receiver
Wire
Inner ear
Microphone
Outer ear
Electrodes
Cable to and from speech processor

implantation. The result was the Medtronic Pacemaker, a compact, battery-powered pulse generator. Today's version is the Medtronic Legend, which exchanges feedback with an external programmer—so that the system may be fine-tuned and programmed to respond to the patient's activity pattern.

While the heart pacemaker is used to stimulate the most essential muscle in the body, even tiny muscles can play an important role in well-being and survival. The ability to control urine flow, for example, depends on the cooperation of the pudendal nerve, the bladder and the bladder's sphincter muscle. This cooperative control may be lost as a result of trauma or aging, leading to urinary incontinence. Searching for a treatment, California researchers have been carrying out experiments involving electronic bladder pacemakers with electrodes implanted in the sacral nerves, which carry information to and from the bladder.

Electrical stimulation is also used for treating the curvature of the spine, known as scoliosis. For the last 20 years doctors have been stimulating the back muscles to strengthen them, an important step in correcting this spinal curvature. Some

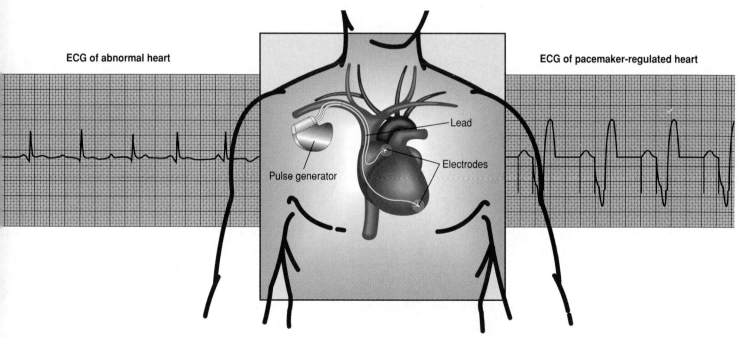

ECG of abnormal heart

ECG of pacemaker-regulated heart

Lead

Pulse generator

Electrodes

doctors prefer to implant a system that runs on a nine-volt battery; others use an external stimulator which is similar to the transcutaneous electrical nerve stimulation system, except for the duration of the electrical pulses and the placement of the electrodes.

Another exciting new use of electricity aids in the rehabilitation of paralyzed patients with spinal cord injury—SCI. When the spinal cord is damaged, the brain cannot send messages to the body—a quadriceps muscle in the leg, for example. Although a message can be initiated and the muscle could still potentially function, the message simply does not arrive, causing paralysis. Now researchers are developing a way to bypass the damaged spinal circuit by sending signals from an electrical stimulator directly to electrodes that are implanted in the muscle, or placed on the skin over the point where the nerve enters the muscle. Electrical impulses from the stimulator cause the paralyzed muscle to contract—similar to an able-bodied person's activity. Sending computer-controlled electrical impulses into various leg muscles for minutes at a time permits a paraplegic or quadriplegic to pedal a modified bicycle, or lift weights. Although this method of rehabilitation is not a cure, it improves physical fitness, health and functional independence.

The principle of delivering electrical messages to the limb also has revolutionized the development of prosthetics, providing an alternative to metal hooks and peg legs. A person who has had an arm amputated, for example, can now be fitted with a battery-powered arm equipped with a hand capable of grasping. The device, called the myoelectric arm, fits snugly over the end of the remnant limb; built-in electrodes make contact with still-healthy muscle. By tensing his biceps in precise ways, learned through biofeedback, the patient causes the remnant muscle to emit bursts of electricity—sometimes no stronger than 15 millionths of a volt. The artificial arm's electrodes pick up the signal and amplify it 1,000 times, sending it through a sophisticated electronic circuit inside the myoelectric forearm. A rechargeable battery activates a small motor that opens or closes the hand or moves the elbow, depending on which muscles the patient has tensed. Researchers are now working on further advancements—notably the sense of touch and five-finger movement—and plan to incorporate computers into the myoelectric design. In future, the arm may have greater smoothness of movement and improved pinch control—a capacity most people take for granted as they reach to pick up a glass of water or squeeze a lemon.

An example of a state-of-the-art limb is the Utah myoelectric arm, so called because it was developed by a company in that state. The prosthesis operates quietly and permits the wearer to move it quickly; the elbow can be locked in position—at up to 22 different angles—allowing the wearer to hold up to 50 pounds. The arm can produce approximately 2,500 elbow flexions on a single charge of the battery module. It has both motorized and mechanical joints and is designed to accept any future updated models that would allow it to rotate at the shoulder. There are several optional attachments, one of which has a rotating wrist and is covered with a glove, creating a more lifelike appearance.

Meanwhile, today's prosthetic legs look so convincing and operate with such smooth efficiency that often they are mistaken for the real thing. One artificial leg, a six-pound prosthesis with a bendable knee, permitted an American high-fashion model to continue her career after losing a leg to cancer. Designed by U.S. prosthetist John Sabolich, the same design can now be equipped with pressure-sensitive sensors that transmit electrical impulses to the skin of the remaining limb, enabling the user to "feel" the floor.

The Sabolich-designed foot is one of the first artificial feet to duplicate many of the functions of a real foot. On contact with the ground, the back part of the arch gives way in order to cushion the body; it then rebounds, recoiling with the same amount of energy the person has just put into the step, lifting him up and forward onto the front part of the arch in readiness for the next step. The foot imitates the arch design of the human foot and is made of space-age composite materials that are strong, light and springy. Now, even people who have lost both legs and feet can walk and run.

Replacement body parts, whether natural organ or tissue transplants, artificial organs or prosthetics, almost appear to work miracles. In fact, what they offer is something most people take for granted: a normal life.

HEART PACEMAKER

Heart conditions involving unusual rhythms—such as erratic signaling between the heart chambers, as shown in the electrocardiogram, or ECG, at left—can be regulated with a pacemaker. Contraction of any muscle is triggered by an electrical impulse; a pacemaker can elicit heart contraction by direct electrical stimulation of the muscle. A normal rhythm is displayed in the ECG at right. As well as the conventional wave pattern reflecting normal heart contractions, the ECG at right shows an extra vertical line with each beat, evidence of the pacemaker's electrical impulse. Consisting of a pulse generator and an electric lead, the heart pacemaker uses miniature electronics to regulate heartbeat. The pulse generator is made up of a battery and an electronic circuit that produces an electrical impulse strong enough to trigger contraction; the lead carries impulses from the pulse generator to one or two electrodes in the heart muscle and back again, allowing the pulse generator to monitor aberrations in the natural rhythm and stimulate a regular heart rhythm.

Walking Tall

Stepping unassisted into a bathtub, picking up a telephone receiver, cooking and eating a meal: Most people take such simple physical activities for granted, yet for thousands of physically handicapped individuals—including those equipped with prosthetic devices—these activities are possible only through individualized training, directed by specialists in rehabilitation medicine. Professionals in this field take medicine beyond its basic mandates—survival and health; their aim is to make a fulfilling life available to all.

An important branch of rehabilitation medicine, called physiotherapy, employs muscle-strengthening techniques to aid paralysis victims, bedridden patients whose muscles have wasted through disuse, and amputees equipped with new artificial limbs. Patients methodically practice techniques of basic survival, the way other individuals might invest time and energy to master a musical instrument. A person with a new prosthetic leg, for example, must relearn the art of walking; coached by a professional called a physiotherapist, the patient practices with the aid of hip-level parallel bars.

While physiotherapy concentrates mainly on gross motor control, the branch of rehabilitation medicine called occupational therapy focuses among other things, on fine motor control and hand-eye coordination. An occupational therapist helps the patient reintegrate into society by teaching job skills and new ways to cope around the house in daily activities; patients recovering from strokes, for example, often need to relearn simple tasks such as cooking a meal.

Once denied handicapped people, so-called everyday activities are now everyday miracles for many.

A bilateral leg amputee runs on prostheses after many hours of physiotherapy exercises. In a tribute to the human will, handicapped individuals participate frequently in sports that allow them to take risks and extend boundaries.

A state-of-the-art artificial arm (above) permits its user to write; minute electrical impulses in the arm signal the fingers to grip the pen and move it on the page. High-tech bioengineering is only part of the story, though; occupational therapists teach patients the muscular coordination required to carry out these fine movements.

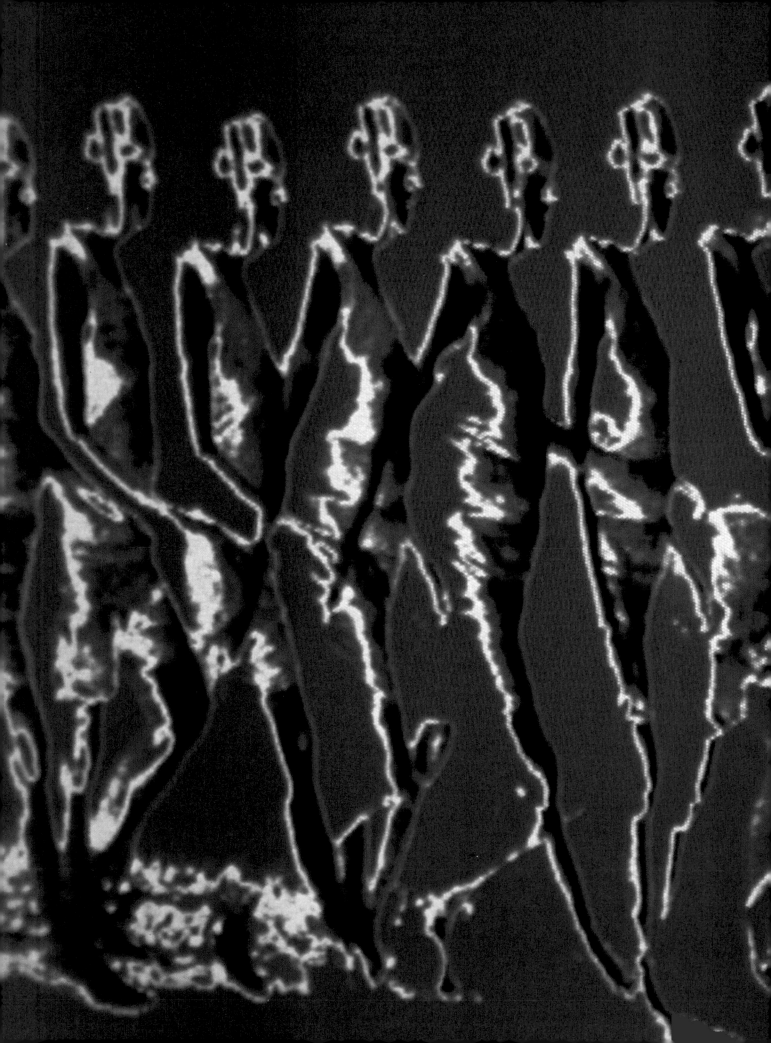

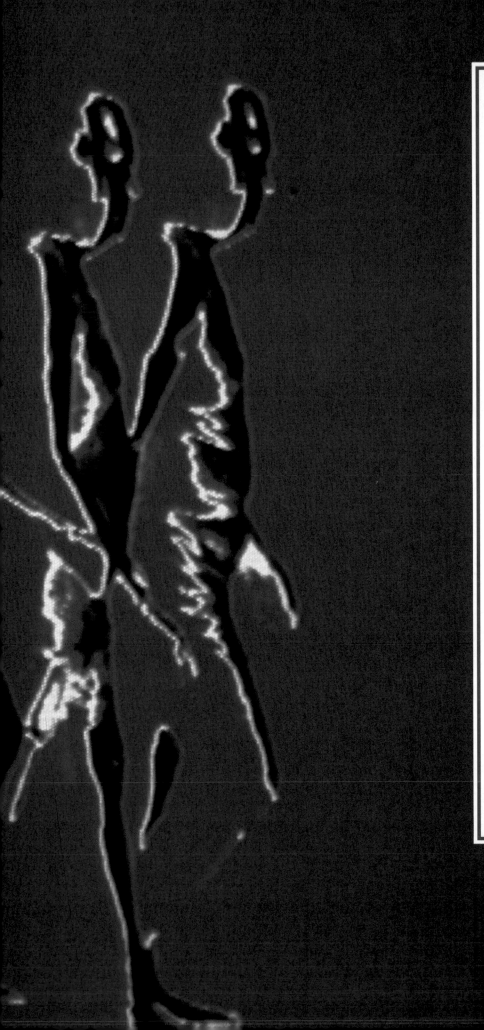

Ode to Immortality

Since earliest times, visions of centaurs, mermaids, and a host of other half-human, half-animal creatures have become deeply established in the human psyche. The fact that these images of life evolved from the fertile recesses of human imagination may reveal that humans accept the idea that they are evolving creatures whose form can be altered.

Developments in biology, occurring almost daily, are aimed at piecing together the jig-saw puzzle of human genetics. In the process, medicine is broadening beyond its conceptual framework of focusing on the gross anatomy of organs, the workings of cells and biochemical routes in the body, and is entering an era of biological alchemy.

This emerging orientation may be a far distance from recreating Man, but molecular scientists believe that new knowledge of how genes repair and replace themselves will provide the keys to a better understanding of human growth and aging, and, in turn, generate medical strategies to slow down the body's deterioration. Already test-tube technology can produce life-like skin, now being used experimentally in the treatment of burns. It appears that the body is becoming the "oyster" of scientists, who are intent on doing away with today's artificial organ and transplant technology in favor of creating organ equivalents in test tubes.

In the era of biological alchemy, life itself is becoming another design problem, though where the limits lie is far from clear.

The march of human evolution has entered a new phase. For the first time, humans themselves will play a decisive role in the step-by-step modification of the race.

Spare Body Parts

In a lab in a plain, red-brick building on an industrial street in Cambridge, Massachusetts, scientists at Organogenesis, a cell-biology company, are creating spare body parts. A living skin equivalent already is being clinically tested on burn victims at the Regional Burn Centre of Western Pennsylvania Hospital in Pittsburgh. Laboratory-created arteries, still in the animal testing stage, may eventually be used in patients requiring new arteries during cardiac bypass, for treatment after stroke or to save limbs whose arteries are not functioning. Also under development is a tissue filler for breast reconstruction in cancer patients.

The manufactured skin closely resembles actual skin and is the result of a mixture of living human skin cells and cow collagen, or protein, that acts as scaffolding on which the cells grow. The ingredients reproduce in a culture under ideal conditions, interacting to form a dermis, the innermost component of human skin, and an epidermis, the fully differentiated, multi-layered outer part of the skin. Hundreds of animal tests indicate that the manufactured skin will not be rejected by the body and that it will develop its own blood supply as blood vessels grow into it; scarring is also reduced.

Tubular blood vessels of any desired length are being created by casting layers of cow collagen together with a knitted collagen mesh in a cylindrical mold. Diameters range from 2mm to 10mm. These blood vessels can be both cut and sutured.

Scientists involved in developing living body parts believe that the technological potential now exists to manufacture many organs and tissues for the human body.

The photomicrograph (below) shows a cross section of human skin, magnified 366 times. The strandlike, protective outer layer, called the epidermis, consists of several layers of cells. Cells in the outermost layer, contain keratin—a fibrous protein. The thicker dermis lies below the innermost layer of the epidermis and consists of fibrous connective tissue that contains blood vessels, hair follicles and sweat glands.

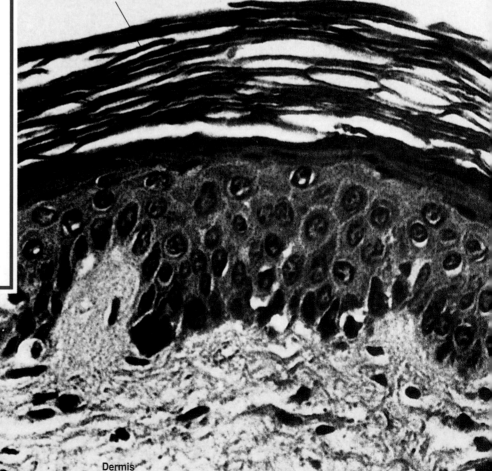

Outermost epidermal layer

Dermis

A scientist inspects a sheet of manufac-tured skin (right), which closely resembles its human counterpart. The skin is pro-duced in a laboratory over a two-month period and can be made in different sizes, shapes and thicknesses.

This photomicrograph (below) shows a cross section of manufactured skin. The human skin equivalent, though it lacks pig-ment cells, hair follicles and sweat glands, is composed of the same epidermal and dermal structures of actual skin.

Outermost epidermal layer

Dermis

Antidote to Aging

As scientists zero in on the cellular processes that accelerate aging, they are discovering important clues to the rules governing lifespan. One theory holds that chemical assassins, known as "free radicals," cause mayhem in vital body cells, leading to their death and, in turn, to the aging and death of the body itself. Free oxygen radicals, the most abundant type affecting humans, are produced during the act of breathing.

Free radicals are highly reactive molecules with an unbalanced complement of electrons—either more or less than the usual number; these free radicals steal electrons from other molecules. The process, called oxidation, is a kind of rusting of cells and occurs in much the same manner as when oxygen rusts metals. This process triggers a destructive chain reaction throughout the body as molecules become unstable and steal electrons from still other molecules. All parts of cells may be damaged, including the genetic material that holds the instructions for making proteins.

Fortunately, the human body is not entirely defenseless. Some natural body enzymes can mop up free radicals and convert them to harmless substances. However, these enzymes diminish with age and medical science is looking to antioxidants that could break up the formation of excessive free radicals. The drug Deprenyl appears to be a possible candidate. To date, it has been used principally to delay the onset of tremors and muscular rigidity in Parkinson's disease, but preliminary animal research shows that Deprenyl also may have an antioxidant effect. Vitamin E is being investigated as another possible antioxidant. Meanwhile, scientists are searching for an even more powerful antioxidant that will extend the human lifespan beyond its present limit of 120 years.

The superoxide radical illustrated at right has an extra electron (colored yellow) that has been stolen from another molecule. A superoxide is one of many free radical molecules that may contribute to aging.

Nucleus
The number of orbiting electrons equals the number of protons in the nucleus so that the overall electrical charge in each atom is zero.

Electron
This particle, which bears a negative electric charge, orbits the atom's nucleus; each oxygen atom normally has eight electrons.

Neutron
This particle, which carries no electric charge, remains in a stable position in the nucleus.

Proton
This particle, which remains in a stable position in the nucleus, bears a positive electric charge equal in magnitude to that of the electron.

Covalent bond
The bond is formed by a shared pair
of electrons, each donated by a separate
atom. The linkage of two oxygen atoms
creates an oxygen molecule—O_2.

Extra electron
The oxygen molecule is made unstable by
the presence of this extra electron. The
resultant chemical unstability is great
enough to pull an electron from another
molecule. This sets off a chain reaction of
"electron stealing," which scientists believe
may lead to the chemical processes associated with aging.

Decoding the Human Body

The longstanding scientific desire to decode the body, molecule by molecule, has led to an international megaproject, launched in 1988, called the human genome project. The human genome—46 chromosomes arranged in 23 pairs in the nucleus of every human cell—contains the genetic instructions that direct life and growth. Chromosomes, sausage-like structures made primarily of deoxyribonucleic acid (DNA), carry all the information necessary to make the human body function. Only four chemical bases—adenine, cytosine, guanine and thymine—run along the length of each DNA molecule; the combinations in which the bases arrange themselves contain codes, many of which tell the cells to produce particular proteins. The goal of the project is to map the location of every gene on the 23 pairs of chromosmes and eventually sequence the three billion DNA bases that make up the human genome. By deciphering the genome, gene by gene, scientists hope to identify the defective chemical bases that cause inherited disorders.

Within a few years, scientists are likely to have the first rough map of where the genes are located on the chromosomes; a decade later, the map may include a sequential and detailed account of the DNA bases. So far, only about 500 genes have been decoded. Even so, this knowledge has led to the identification of what are called genetic markers, red flags for disorders such as cystic fibrosis, Tay-Sachs disease, sickle-cell anemia, muscular dystrophy, and Huntington's chorea. A host of new and powerful diagnostic tests for signs of genetic abnormalities and the emergence of new medical therapies to offset the genetic roots of many diseases are certain to evolve from this knowledge.

In the meantime, the issue of genetic privacy is emerging as the awesome power to read the genetic tea leaves of humankind begins to bear fruit.

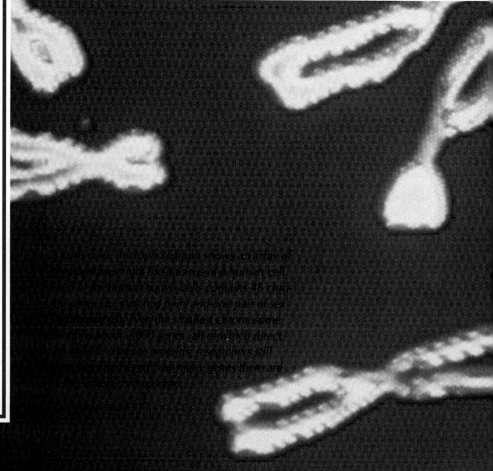

A researcher analyzes a gene on an automated deoxyribonucleic acid (DNA) sequencing machine. Each color on the computer screen represents one of DNA's four kinds of chemical bases, which arrange themselves in an almost infinite variety of sequences in the human genome. The order determines which genetic instructions DNA carries; errors in the order can result in genetic diseases.

Fluorescent spots on a human chromosome, depicted on this computer screen, show either the location of genes or of other markers that are used to pinpoint genes. This technique, called chromosome mapping, allows researchers to locate pieces of DNA directly on chromosomes.

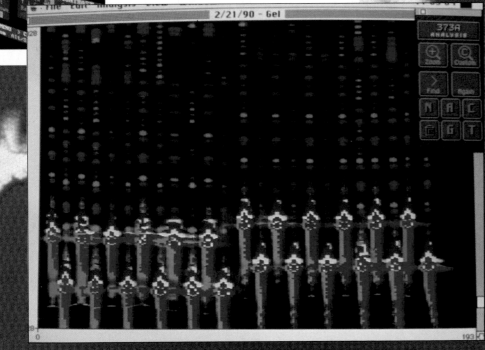

Index

Numerals in *italics* indicate an illustration of the subject mentioned.

PICTURE CREDITS

Multiple credits on a page are read left to right, top to bottom, divided by semicolons.

Cover: Photograph by Barry Blackman, Telegraph Color Library/Masterfile

6 Jerry Valente. 7 Julie Léger. 8,9 © Museo del Prado; Courtesy National Library of Medicine, Bethesda; © Her Majesty Queen Elizabeth II, Windsor Castle, Royal Library; The Bettmann Archive. 10,11 National Library of Medicine, Bethesda; World Health Organization, Geneva; Courtesy Swiss Museum of Pharmaceutical History; National Library of Medicine, Bethesda. 12,13 National Library of Medicine, Bethesda; The William H. Helfand Collection; © Institut Pasteur; Courtesy National Library of Medicine, Bethesda. 14,15 Jerry Valente. 21 Robert Chartier. 22,23 Dr. Owen Beatty/University of Alberta (2). 26,27 Leonard Lessin; Dr. Kenkichi Oho/Peter Arnold. 30 Howard Sochurek. 32 Howard Sochurek. 34 Howard Sochurek. 39 David Frazier/The Stock Market. 42 Manfred Kage/Peter Arnold Inc.; E.S. Anderson/Photo Researchers Inc. 43 Courtesy Electron Microscopy Lab-Pathology Department/Montreal General Hospital. 52 Image from Fran Heyl Associates, SEM by Nina Lampen, computer enhancement by Pix*Elation (2). 60 Philip C. Jackson. 65 University of California, San Francisco/Computer Graphics Laboratory. 66,67 Mark J. Plotkin/Conservation International; Gregory G. Dimijian/Photo Researchers Inc. 68 Martin Rotker/ First Light. 70 Ken Straiton/First Light; Robert Isear/Photo Researchers Inc. 72,73 Philip C. Jackson; Gale K. Belinky/Photo Researchers Inc. 74,75 Vladimir Lange/The Image Bank. 76 Larry Mulvehill/Photo Researchers Inc. 78,79 Patrick McKoy, courtesy Centre Hospitalier Anna-Laberge. 81 T. Park/Medichrome. 83 Brian R. Wolff. 84,85 SIU/Peter Arnold. 87 Steve Chenn/First Light. 88,89 Julie Léger. 90 Courtesy University of California, Davis. 92,93 Courtesy Sunnybrook Health Science Centre, Division of Plastic Surgery (2). 94 Harrington/Masterfile. 95 Phillip Hayson/Photo Researchers Inc. 96 Alexander Tsarias/Photo Researchers Inc. 98,99 Patrick McKoy, courtesy Centre Hospitalier Anna-Laberge. 100,101 Richard Dunoff/The Stock Market. 106,107 Gilles Delisle (2). 102, 103 Courtesy Siemens Canada. 108,109 Patrick McKoy, courtesy Centre Hospitalier Anna-Laberge (2). 110,111 Catherine Urgillo/Photo Researchers Inc. 113 Louis Pshiyos/Matrix International. 114,115 Will & Deni McIntyre/Photo Researchers Inc. 123 Courtesy Dr. Thomas Chang. 125 Ted Tamburo. 130,131 Chuck O'Rear/First Light; Richard Himeisen/Medichrome. 132,133 Howard Sochurek/The Stock Market. 134,135 Courtesy Organogenesis Inc.; Burt Glinn/Magnum.138,139 Howard Sochurek/The Stock Market; Dr. Craig Venter/NIH, courtesy The Human Genome Project; Dr. Glen Evans/The Salk Institute, courtesy The Human Genome Project.

ILLUSTRATION CREDITS

16-19 Shawn Potvin/L. Madore; 62-63 Jean-François Ozenne/L. Madore; 92,93 Courtesy Marie Lehman, Medical Art Department, Sunnybrook Health Science Centre (3). 104, 105 Courtesy Les Architectes Tétrault, Parent, Languedoc et Associés; Courtesy J.L.P. Associés.

ACKNOWLEDGMENTS

The editors wish to thank the following:

Dr. Leon Axel, Department of Radiology, University of Pennsylvania, Philadelphia, PA; Dr. Malcolm G. Baines, Department of Microbiology and Immunology, McGill University, Montreal, Que.; Dr. Allan Barkun, Department of Gastroenterology, Montreal General Hospital, Montreal, Que.; Professor B.W. Barry, School of Pharmacy, University of Bradford, Bradford, West Yorkshire; Dr. Gerald Batist, Department of Oncology, McGill University, Montreal, Que.; Suzanne Bayly, Department of Pharmacology, McGill University, Montreal, Que.; Dr. Geoffrey P. Blake, Department of Hematology, Montreal General Hospital, Montreal, Que.; Stan Booth, Merck Frosst Canada Inc., Kirkland, Que.; Paul Bradbury, B.C. Institute of Technology, Burnaby, B.C.; Doreen Brennan, Bloc Opératoire, Centre Hospitalier Anna-Laberge, Châteauguay, Que.; Dr. Patrice Bret, Department of Radiology, Montreal General Hospital, Montreal, Que.; Dr. Dalius J. Briedis, Department of Microbiology and Immunology, McGill University, Montreal, Que.; Thomas M.S. Chang, Department of Artificial Cells and Organs, McGill University, Montreal, Que.; Claude Choinière, Communications Department, Centre Hospitalier Anna-Laberge, Châteauguay, Que.; Dr. Joe T.R. Clarke, Clinical Genetics, Hospital for Sick Children, Toronto, Ont.; Neil C. Colman, Respiratory Division, Montreal General Hospital, Montreal, Que.; Eugene Daniels, Department of Anatomy, McGill University, Montreal, Que.; Claude Desrosiers, Department of Communications, Urgences Santé Montreal, Que.; Dr. W.P. Duguid, Department of Pathology, Montreal General Hospital, Montreal, Que.; Kim Dziedziula, COBE Cardiovascular Inc. Arvado, Co.; D.J. Ecobichom, Department of Pharmacology and Therapeutics, McGill University, Montreal, Que.; Dr. B. Esplin, Department of Pharmacology and Therapeutics, McGill University, Montreal, Que.; Lise Fournier, Soins Intensifs, Centre Hospitalier Anna-Laberge, Chateauguay, Que.; Dr. Carolyn Freeman, Department of Radiotherapy, Montreal General Hospital, Montreal, Que.; Carol Gillis, Sterling-Winthrop Inc., Aurora, Ont.; Dr. Roger M. Glaser, National Center for Rehabilitation, Wright State University, Dayton, OH; Pierre Godmaire, Fisher Scientific Ltd., Montreal, Que.; Dr. Phil Gold, Department of Medicine, Montreal General Hospital, Montreal, Que.; Dr. Réjeanne Gougeon, Nutrition Department, Royal Victoria Hospital, Montreal, Que.; Dr. Hamilton Hall, Orthopedic and Arthritic Hospital, Toronto, Ontario; Dr. Terry Hambrecht, Department of Neurological Prosthesis, National Institute of Neurological Disorders and Stroke, Bethesda, MD; John P. Harley, Department of Microbiology, Eastern Kentucky University, Richmond, KY.; Dr. Joseph M. Hayes, Transplant Surgeon, Cleveland Clinic, Cleveland, OH; E. John Hinchey, Department of Surgery, Montreal General Hospital, Montreal, Que.; House Ear Institute Public Relations Department, Los Angeles, CA.; Dr. Robert M. Julien, Department of Anesthesiology, St. Vincent Hospital, Portland, OR; Dr. Joel S. Karp, Department of Radiology, University of Pennsylvania, Philadelphia, PA.; Dr. Albert S. Lyons, History of Medicine, Mount Sinai School of Medicine, Toronto, Ont.; Margrethe May, Allied Health Division, Delta College, Bay City, MI; Elizabeth McClosky, Hemodialysis Department, Dialysis Unit, Montreal General Hospital, Montreal, Que.; Shirlyn Mckenzie, University of Texas Health Science Center, San Antonio, TX; Dr. Ian Metcalf, Department of Anesthesiology, Montreal General Hospital, Montreal, Que.; Dr. A.E. Mgebroff, Yoakum Medical Clinic, Yoakum, TX; Laura Mills, Department of Public Affairs, Alza Corporation, Palo Alto, CA; Dr. JD Mortensen, Cardiopulmonics, Salt Lake City, UT; Sheshadri Narayanan; National Center for Human Genome Reserach, Bethesda, MD.; Dr. John A. Oliver, Department of Urology, Royal Victoria Hospital, Montreal, Que.; Dr. George M. Pantalos, Artificial Heart Research Laboratory, University of Utah, Salt Lake City, UT; Serge Perras, Les Architectes Tétrault, Parent, Languedoc et Associés, Montreal, Que.; Dr. John Phillips, Division of Plastic Surgery, Sunnybrook Health Science Centre, Toronto, Ont.; Mark Plotkin, Conservation International, Washington D.C.; Dr. Judes Poirier, Douglas Hospital, Verdun, Que.; Yves Pouliot, General Electric Medical Systems, St. Laurent, Que.; Dick Reid, Medtronic Inc., Minneapolis, MN; Bernard Robaire, Department of Pharmacology and Therapeutics, McGill University, Montreal, Que.; Thomas D. Rohde, Department of Surgery, University of Minnesota Health Center, Minneapolis, MN; Lawrence Rosenberg, Department of Surgery, Montreal General Hospital, Montreal, Que.; Michael D. Rosengarten, Department of Cardiology, Montreal General Hospital, Montreal, Que.; Leonard Rosenthall, Department of Nuclear Medicine, Montreal General Hospital, Montreal, Que.; Paul Sauvageau, J.L.P. et associes, Montreal, Que.; Harold H. Sears, Motion Control Inc., Salt Lake City, UT; Dr. Peter J. Somerville, Department of Nephrology, Montreal General Hospital, Montreal, Que.; Paul-André Tétrault, Les Architectes Tétrault, Parent, Languedoc et Associés, Montreal, Que.; Dr. Martin Veilleux, McGill University, Montreal, Que.; Lawrence L. Weed, PKC Corporation, South Burlington, VT; Dr. Jeffrey C. Weinreb, Division of Magnetic Resonance Imaging, NYU Medical Center, New York, NY; Dr. H. Bruce Williams, Division of Plastic and Reconstructive Surgery, Montreal General Hospital, Montreal, Que.; Carol Sorrels-Yandell, Department of Communications, Sabolich Prosthetics and Research Center, Oklahoma City, OK; Ioannis V. Yannas, Department of Mechanical Engineering, Massachusetts Institute of Technology, Cambridge, MA.

The following persons also assisted in the preparation of this book:
Sari Berger, Graphor Consultations, Jenny Meltzer, Shirley Sylvain.

This book was designed on Apple Macintosh® computers, using QuarkXPress® in conjunction with CopyFlow/CopyBridge™ and a Linotronic® 300R for page layout and composition; StrataVision 3d.®, Adobe Illustrator 88® and Adobe Photoshop® were used as illustration programs.